# MUSHROOMS

# MUSHROOMS
## A Natural and Cultural History

Nicholas P. Money

REAKTION BOOKS

Published by Reaktion Books Ltd
Unit 32, Waterside
44–48 Wharf Road
London N1 7UX, UK

www.reaktionbooks.co.uk

First published 2017
Paperback edition first published 2022
Copyright © Nicholas P. Money 2017

Printed and bound in India by Replika Press Pvt. Ltd

A catalogue record for this book is available from the British Library

ISBN 978 1 78914 616 5

# Contents

Pair of fruit bodies of a gilled mushroom.

# Introduction

Soft umbrellas
of the underworld
push up
through beaded moss,
spokes rusted with spores,
eager for wind
CHRISTINE BOYKA KLUGE, 'Toadstools'[1]

Mushrooms are loved, despised, feared and misunderstood. This is true of many other groups of organisms – sharks are loved, despised and so on – but the fruit bodies of fungi occupy a special place in human consciousness, embedded in childhood through fairy tales, films and video games. Widespread familiarity with mushrooms provides an audience for the study of fungi, or mycology, but a great deal of remedial work is necessary to counter misconceptions about these fascinating organisms. This book introduces mushroom mythology and science, the history of our interactions with these fungi, and the ways in which humans use mushrooms as food, medicine and recreational drugs. The natural history is supplemented with profiles of the mycologists who advanced the study of the fungi. As paragons of eccentricity, these individuals are peerless.

A mushroom is not a self-contained organism, like a jellyfish, for example. It is a reproductive organ produced by a colony, or mycelium, which grows in soil or rotting wood. For convenience, we use the term 'mushroom' rather than 'mushroom-forming fungus' to describe the whole organism, although this is a bit like using a photograph of a large pair of testicles to represent an elephant. Describing the fungi that form mushrooms as micro-organisms may seem strange given the macroscopic nature of their fruit bodies. It is justified, however, because mushrooms tend to be short-lived compared with the continuous feeding activities of the microscopic filaments of their supporting mycelia. There is no ambiguity in the inclusion of other fungi within the purview of microbiology, because they do not form mushrooms, and go unnoticed without magnification.

Mushrooms are produced by 16,000 species of fungi classified as basidiomycetes. They grow on every continent, thriving in wet conditions, breaking down organic matter and recycling soil nutrients. Mushrooms also support trees and shrubs through root connections called mycorrhizas, in tropical, temperate and boreal ecosystems. An equivalent number of basidiomycetes grow as budding yeasts, and rusts and smuts that attack plants. The basidiomycetes are one of a handful of major categories of fungi. The others include ascomycetes, 'pin moulds' that spoil food, and a spectacular range of aquatic fungi whose spores swim like animal sperm cells. More than 70,000 species of fungi have been described and those awaiting discovery probably run into the millions. This mismatch between known and unknown results from the astonishing richness of microscopic organisms, our inability to grow most of them in Petri dishes, and significant problems with sorting out species of fungi. The straightforward differences that enable us to discriminate between foxes and rabbits do not apply to mushrooms, and we are left with many 'species' that may or may not be separate entities.

Mushrooms have been the subject of superstition and folklore for centuries and they were objects of worship by ancient civilizations. The association between mushrooms and varied fancies is explained, in part, by their strangeness. The overnight appearance of mushrooms is a startling phenomenon and the growth of some species in 'fairy' rings seems very peculiar until one understands

Mid-16th-century woodcut of mushrooms with a pair of snakes and a snail.

how they grow. Other superstitions, including their associations with witchcraft, derive from the poisonous and hallucinogenic natures of a small number of species.

Rational approaches to the study of mushrooms began with the work of Renaissance botanists in the sixteenth century, and fungi were presented in the great European herbals of this era. The first sensible guide to mushroom edibility was published in 1675, and mushroom colonies were featured in the work of the early microscopists. At this time, mushrooms were regarded as a peculiar branch of the animal kingdom, something akin to sponges or worms. This is interesting given current molecular evidence of shared ancestry between fungi and animals. In the eighteenth century most authorities viewed fungi as primitive plants, which explains why mycology is treated as a branch of botany when zoology is a more logical fit for these animal relatives.

Pier Antonio Micheli was the first naturalist to conduct experiments on mushrooms, and his *Nova plantarum genera*, published in 1729, is a masterpiece of early scientific investigation. He died from pleurisy in 1737, contracted during a mushroom-collecting trip, and is remembered as 'the father of mycology'. Micheli was the first of a remarkable succession of eccentrics who have dedicated their lives to the study of mushrooms. Foremost among the historical figures is A. H. Reginald Buller, a British-born scientist who was a founding member of the science faculty at the University of Manitoba in the early twentieth century. He lived in hotels in Winnipeg for forty years and crossed the Atlantic each summer to work at Kew. A lifelong bachelor, with singular dedication to mycology, Buller walked to work with horse blinders strapped to his head to preserve his light sensitivity for experiments on bioluminescent mushrooms. He was attacked by an eagle while collecting mushrooms with students, and wrote dreadful poems about fungi in his leisure hours. His American counterpart, Curtis Gates Lloyd, was similarly obsessed. This wealthy Cincinnati bachelor published a mycological journal for 28 years and used his uncontested editorials to ridicule the work of prominent academics with whom he warred.

Lloyd's peculiarities are eclipsed, perhaps, by the work of Captain Charles McIlvaine, veteran of the American Civil War, novelist and poet. In pursuit of the greatest mushroom guide in history, McIlvaine volunteered as his own experimental animal, testing the edibility of every mushroom described in his *One Thousand American Fungi* (1900). This enormous tome is testament to a man's triumph over unappetizing stews and digestive discomfort. The peculiarities of women mycologists pale in comparison with these gentlemen of the science, which is not surprising given the greater tolerance of male eccentricity within society.

Through the endeavours of Buller and his contemporaries, we learned that mushrooms were far stranger and much more interesting than anything imagined in mycological folklore. Other mycologists were satisfied with identifying fungi, but Buller revealed the beauty of the microscopic activity beneath mushroom caps that allow single fruit bodies to release billions of spores in a day. Multiplied by the immense numbers of fruit bodies in the world's forests, this astonishing fecundity mists the atmosphere with millions of tons of spores, causing misery for asthmatics, affecting atmospheric chemistry and even influencing rainfall patterns.

Research in many other fields has advanced the science of mushroom biology in recent decades. Ecologists who study the below-ground colonies that produce mushrooms have shown how these fungi support the growth of trees and shrubs through mycorrhizal associations. In a mycorrhiza, the mushroom colony, or mycelium, forms tight gloves over root tips and supplies water and dissolved minerals to the plant in return for sugars produced by photosynthesis. Other ecological studies have shown the critical role of mushroom mycelia in plant disease and wood decay. Using the phenomenal magnifying power of the electron

Clouds of spores drifting from fruit bodies of the common ink cap, *Coprinopsis atramentaria*.

microscope and advances in light microscopy, mycologists have explored the mechanisms that allow filamentous cells called hyphae to grow at their tips and branch to form mycelia. And, lastly, the application of molecular methods to study evolutionary relationships between species has provided the basis for a natural scheme of mushroom classification that reflects kinship rather than superficial similarities in appearance. Investigations in all of these areas will be discussed in this book.

Interest in identifying, picking and eating mushrooms has grown alongside these scientific investigations, and 'mushrooming' has become a hobby that attracts enthusiasts of all ages. These amateur mycologists are blessed with the knowledge that an autumn foray in the woods is among life's greatest pleasures. Mushroom identification can be very tricky and expert practitioners draw on information from many sources to pin down a species. In the field, where one is limited to viewing the shape, size and colour of a fruit body, and inhaling its perfume, the location of the fungus becomes important. The development of a mushroom on a hardwood or softwood log, or its growth beside a particular species of tree, is an important clue to its identity. This broader view of mushroom biology, where we consider the fruit body as a participant in the life of a forest rather than an insulated entity, is an important theme in this book.

If the decision is made to pick for the kitchen, the art of mushroom cookery can develop into a lifelong passion. The ancient Greeks were unenthusiastic about mushrooms, but Roman gourmets embraced their strong flavours two thousand years ago. Juvenal and other classical writers referred to the glories of the mushrooms served to the most important guests at banquets, and we can attempt to reproduce these dishes today. Wild mushrooms have more cachet on restaurant menus than cultivated species, but they account for a tiny fraction of mushroom sales compared with white button mushrooms, grown on compost, and shiitake, raised on logs. China has become the world leader in the cultivation of both mushroom species, and more wild mushrooms are harvested from forests in China than any other country.

Mushrooms have a Jekyll and Hyde nature. The majority of mushrooms are harmless, as McIlvaine proved in 1900, but a few highly toxic species have killed consumers for millennia. Most poisonings are due to mistaken identification rather than deliberate assassination or suicide attempts. The only good thing to say about the worst mushroom poisonings is that victims today with access to modern medical care may survive by virtue of dialysis or organ transplant. Mushroom toxicity is part of a much wider set of physiological reactions to the consumption of fruit bodies. Claims about the medicinal value of mushrooms have a long history, but there is little evidence of their efficacy of the kind that we demand of drugs developed by the pharmaceutical industry. Prospects for finding useful compounds in mushrooms seem good, however, when we consider the biochemical complexity of fruit bodies. Like toxins, psilocybin and other psychotropic molecules are examples of compounds that have profound effects on human physiology. Beyond the entertainment value of psychedelic mushrooms there is growing interest in the way that psilocybin affects the brain. Research suggests that this strange metabolite might be useful in the treatment of clinical depression and can alleviate fear among patients with terminal illnesses.

In this time of constant awareness of our deep impact on the health of the biosphere, the sustainability of wild mushroom populations is ignored by most scientists and political activists engaged in conservation. This is not surprising given public interest in endangered animals, but climate change, industrial pollution, deforestation and other causes of habitat destruction threaten fungi as much as any other organism. Overharvesting of wild mushrooms is another troubling and controversial issue that requires objective consideration. Life on land has always depended on the ecological activities of mushrooms. Forests and grasslands would collapse without the support of healthy populations of fungi.

Growing appreciation of the significance of mushrooms has led to the idea that the deliberate cultivation of mycelia may help to restore land damaged by human activity. Promising research has demonstrated how fungi can purify soils polluted by industrial waste, help to re-establish trees and rehabilitate land ravaged by mining operations. The translation of these experiments into workable methods of environmental remediation is a formidable scientific challenge.

*one*

# Mushroom Superstition

**M**ushrooms fruited in the forests and grasslands occupied by our hominid ancestors and have been a familiar part of nature throughout human history. In the modern urban environment, where wild mushrooms are scarce, popular culture has maintained our awareness of fungi. The earliest references to mushrooms come from Greek and Roman authors concerned with their edibility.[1] Fragments of Greek writings refer to the dangers of eating fungi rather than celebrating their uses in the kitchen. In the fifth century BC, Euripides wrote an epigram about a family poisoned by mushrooms, and Hippocrates warned against eating raw fruit bodies. In the first century AD, Dioscorides recommended a precautionary vomit after a dinner containing mushrooms, and Pliny the Elder wondered what great pleasure could be obtained from eating 'such a risky food'.[2] These judgements were widely ignored and the Roman taste for mushrooms is evident from recipes that pre-date Pliny, and from frescoes uncovered at Herculaneum showing fresh mushrooms on a kitchen shelf.

Mushroom poisoning is an obvious source of superstition about fungi. When we add the sudden appearance of fruit bodies, their phallic shape, hallucinogenic properties and bioluminescence, the development of irrational ideas about mushrooms does not seem at all surprising. We are fortunate to live at a time when all of these phenomena can be approached rationally. Science can provide a richer appreciation of mushrooms than anyone imagined 'across the vast gulf of the monkish and deluded past'.[3] Long-standing superstitions are interesting, however, because they highlight common-sense questions about mushrooms: what are they and where do they come from?

The overnight appearance of mushrooms on a lawn can be a delightful discovery, even for someone with no interest in cooking them. Plants tend to lack this way of surprising us. They grow more slowly and although some flowers open swiftly, we expect them to burst from their buds. Mushrooms develop from buried primordia and some species expand from multilayered eggs. Sliced open, the eggs reveal miniature mushrooms with unexpanded stems, caps and gills. Handled gently, these will hatch in a dish at home if they are kept moist. *Amanita* species have beautiful egg stages. The emergence of the orange cap of Caesar's mushroom, *Amanita caesarea*, from its white membrane is very striking. When mushrooms have a particularly phallic appearance, their enlargement can be met with amazement. The common stinkhorn, *Phallus impudicus*, and its relatives, offer the additional shock of delivering appalling smells. From a distance of a few metres, the scent of a stinkhorn is like that of a rotting animal. Up very close to the slimy head of the fruit body, the perfume is more complex and sickening, and can leave one feeling light-headed and nauseated. There is nothing quite like it. The rich folklore inspired by phallic mushrooms is evident in their common names, which include devil's eggs, devil's horns and devil's stinkpot.[4] Anything this rude must be the work of the Devil! In Nigerian traditions, stinkhorns are associated with death and are used to make charms that can protect the user or curse an enemy.[5] Western folklore about stinkhorns is milder, with their appearance signifying the work of evil spirits to some commentators and attracting others to their hopeful application as aphrodisiacs.

Fairy rings have encouraged a lot of folklore. A number of mushroom species that are common in meadows fruit in conspicuous circles and produce rings of luxuriant green grass. Some fungi create a thin ring of dead grass within the band of brightened vegetation and others fruit in a halo without seeming to affect the grass at all. Fairy rings also develop in forests. The association between fairy rings and fairies probably seems obvious to anyone

Caesar's mushroom, *Amanita caesarea*, emerging from its egg stage.

brought up on fairy tales, but it is interesting to consider how these ideas developed in the first place. The symmetry of fairy rings is an obvious stimulus. Large circles in grass suggest some form of deliberate husbandry and in the absence of an obvious craftsperson it is easy to imagine a supernatural agent at work. The same notions developed in the 1980s when all manner of bizarre claims were made about the origin of crop circles before they were recognized as hoaxes. Without a rational explanation for a natural phenomenon, our thoughts tend to slide towards the fantastical.

If rings of mushrooms are occupied by pixies, sprites or elves, it seems reasonable to wonder whether these creations pose a danger to us, or might be places where wishes are granted. And this has led people to tell tales of kidnapping reminiscent of modern stories of alien abduction, and of terrible spells cast on the unwary who have entered the torus of green grass. On the positive side, morning dew collected from a ring was described

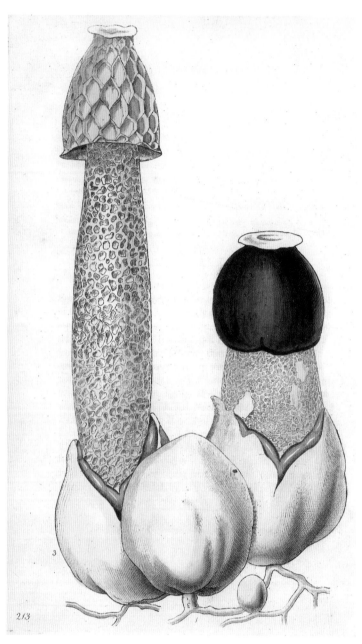

Common stinkhorn, *Phallus impudicus*, shown as a pea-sized primordium, in its larger egg phase, as the emergent fruit body carrying malodorous spore slime, and as an erect fruit body with slime removed by flies.

as an effective love potion and, in an associated strain, was said to improve a girl's complexion. The influence of mushrooms is conveyed in these excerpts from 'The Fairy Ring', a light verse published in 1863:

> I have got a wish the maiden said,
> Then merrily off to the woods she sped –
> A gay and gladsome, joyous thing –
> To wish it in the fairy ring.
> . . .
> And was her wish granted by the fay?
> Indeed, and indeed, I cannot say:
> But when next that way I wound
> There came the church-bells' merry sound.[6]

Earlier beliefs about fairy rings may have factored in the design of Neolithic stone circles in Europe. The historical use of

Fairy ring of fruit bodies of *Clitocybe nebularis*, whose spores have whitewashed the vegetation.

Part of the King's Men circle, one of the three Neolithic and Bronze Age monuments of the Rollright Stones in Oxfordshire.

these monuments in religious practices is unknown, but their resemblance to fairy rings seems clear. According to this idea, Stonehenge could be an example of extravagant biomimicry, but we need to be cautious. It is tempting to think that the magnificent King's Men stone circle, one of three monuments that form the Rollright Stones in Oxfordshire, reflects the mycological inspiration of its prehistoric architects. This interpretation is wrong, however, because archaeologists have found that today's separated stones were fashioned by centuries of weathering of an original unbroken enclosure.

In Germany, fairy rings are associated with the assembly of witches on Walpurgisnacht (30 April), and according to French mythology, enormous toads with bulging eyes appear in fairy rings, or *ronds de sorcières,* and are capable of great malevolence. Edmund Spenser makes the amphibian connection in *The Shepheardes Calender* of 1579, where 'paddocks' refers to toads: 'The grieslie Todestoole growne there mought I see / And loathed paddocks lording on the same.'[7]

The relationship between toads and toadstools has obscure roots, but we can make some sensible guesses about its origin. The slimy skin of toads and the surface of mushroom caps is an obvious link and the appearance of amphibians and fruit bodies in wet weather is another convergence. The connection is strengthened by the poisonous nature of a few species in both groups, their supposed incorporation in witches' potions, and confusion about the spontaneous generation of both tadpoles and mushrooms. It is interesting that the connection between toads (and frogs) and mushrooms is not just a European phenomenon, but also exists

Copy of an 18th-century woodcut showing 'the little people' dancing in a ring beside a mushroom. The little people live in the molehill, shown at left, from which they emerge to dance on moonlit nights.

in Africa, Asia and Central America. The origin of 'mushroom' is more mysterious, with ambiguous connections to moss, mucus and foam or froth (*mousse* in French).[8] The last of these possibilities is supported by Pliny's contention that mushrooms begin 'flimsier than froth' and develop from 'slime and the souring juice of the damp ground, or often of the root of acorn-bearing trees.'[9]

Some naturalists have reserved the word 'toadstool' for poisonous species, regarding the greater diversity of fruit bodies as 'mushrooms', but there is no consensus on this point.[10] These distinctions are impossible to maintain because many writers extended the term 'toadstool' to many harmless fruit body forms, including jelly fungi, puffballs, earth-stars, bracket fungi and phallic mushrooms. It is simplest to say that all fruit bodies of basidiomycete fungi are mushrooms. This definition seems to be most common today. Toadstools are on their way to obsolescence.

Traditional beliefs about identifying poisonous species are terribly dangerous for pickers who entrust their lives to the claim that toxic mushrooms tarnish silver spoons or that any type of fruit body nibbled by other animals is safe for humans. Neither claim is true. There is no guide to edibility other than learning how to identify any mushroom that you are considering for dinner or trusting an expert to do so. Thankfully, it is not very difficult to avoid the really nasty species, but people make dreadful mistakes with mushrooms each year.

The neurological effects elicited by psychotropic compounds in magic mushrooms are among the most important sources of superstitions about fungi. *Psilocybe* mushrooms were consumed by Aztec priests in religious ceremonies and the fly agaric, *Amanita muscaria*, has served as an intoxicant in Russia for centuries. Accounts of fly agaric use in Siberia and the Russian Far East by European explorers inspired scenes in Lewis Carroll's *Alice's Adventures in Wonderland*, including Alice's shrinking after tasting the Caterpillar's mushroom, and earlier European folklore kindled varied fantasies about fungi.[11] There are very few facts

The fly agaric, *Amanita muscaria.*

about the historical use of magic mushrooms and this has led some enthusiasts to pursue wild imaginative journeys. Contrary to the more extravagant hypotheses, Christianity did not grow from a cult of mushroom worship, and it is impossible to decipher the symbolic meaning of mushrooms in Neolithic cave paintings.

Bioluminescence is another mycological phenomenon that has inspired irrational beliefs about fungi. More than seventy species of mushroom glow with a bluish-green light that is visible at night. In some species, both the fruit bodies and supporting colonies emit light. Bioluminescent colonies feeding on rotting wood produce a glow known as 'foxfire'. Aristotle described this 'cold fire' associated with wood, and Pliny described a white mushroom that 'is phosphorescent at night'. Colonies of the honey fungus, *Armillaria mellea*, and related species are probably responsible for references to foxfire in European literature. Stories have been told about soldiers in the trenches of the First World War sticking pieces of luminescent wood in their helmet webbing to make themselves visible to fellow soldiers in the dark without attracting enemy snipers.[12] Fruit bodies and colonies of the jack-o'-lantern,

Bioluminescent species of *Gerronema* growing in the Atlantic Forest in the Brazilian state of São Paulo. Left, photograph taken using headlamp. Right, photograph taken in darkness using a 21-minute camera exposure.

*Omphalotus illudens*, and the bitter oyster, *Panellus stipticus*, emit a dim green light. Brighter mushrooms are more common in warm, wet climates, and tropical rainforests are alight with them. Girls in New Caledonia have used them as hair ornaments, and children in the neighbouring islands of Vanuatu illuminate themselves with sticky fruit bodies. Exploring Ambon in Indonesia in the seventeenth century, the Dutch botanist Rumphius described a gilled mushroom he called 'the fiery campernoyle':

> At night they are lit like stars, alight with blue fire . . . the natives carry [the fungus] in their hands at night, in order to show their followers with this fire where the front man is going . . . but they will only do this from necessity . . . imagining that [the lights] are the Sorcerers [who] go about at night with a glowing head, and mislead those who follow them.[13]

Mushroom superstitions are global.

Some mushrooms are delicious, others can poison us; they appear overnight and can grow in rings; they have curious shapes;

some are brightly coloured and some have horrible smells; a few cause hallucinations and others glow in the dark. It is no wonder that mushrooms are viewed as a magical part of nature. In the next chapter we go beyond the imaginary and consider the ways in which science began to untangle the peculiarities of fungi that form mushrooms.

Sixteenth-century woodcut of agarikon, *Laricifomes officinalis*, fruiting on larch trees.

*two*

# Mushroom Science

Pliny and other natural historians of the classical era were concerned with the edibility and medicinal properties of mushrooms and commented on the geographical distribution of the most sought-after species. These writers treated fungi with caution and nothing was learned about the nature of mushrooms until the end of the medieval period. The scientific exploration of mycology began with investigations by the Italian botanists of the Renaissance.[1] In the sixteenth century, Pietro Andrea Mattioli provided the earliest illustrations of fungi that can be identified with confidence, and Andrea Cesalpino included descriptions of mushroom development in his book *De plantis libri*. Cesalpino regarded fungi as transitional life forms that shared features of plants and animals and emerged from decaying matter. Illustrated descriptions of mushrooms by Mathias de l'Obel in the 1580s were copied and augmented by seventeenth-century botanists, and early mycological knowledge emerged as a splendid mishmash of art and science.

Giambattista della Porta described 'seeds, very small and black' produced by mushrooms in 1588. Since mushroom spores are microscopic and the microscope had not been invented when he made this deduction, it is likely that he was looking at clumps or dustings of spores collected from fruit bodies. More than a century would pass before the generation of fungi from spores was established. Meanwhile, the development of the microscope in the early seventeenth century led to the realization that mushrooms were related to an incredible diversity of fungi that had been known only as blotches on leaves and hairiness on rotting fruit. Robert Hooke's engravings of microscopic fungi in his *Micrographia* of 1665 were the first illustrations of any microorganism.

Hooke also looked at mushrooms with his microscope and discovered that they were made from masses of branching and interwoven filaments. It is easy enough to repeat this observation today by teasing apart a tiny piece of a mushroom stem in a drop of water on a glass slide. Modern microscopes, even the least expensive models, provide a much clearer view of the filaments than Hooke enjoyed. But although the parallel walls of these cylindrical cells, called hyphae, can be brought into sharp focus, we are little closer today to understanding how the shapes of different mushrooms emerge from these tangled strands. There is a simplicity and

Robert Hooke's engraving of the microscopic fungus *Mucor* growing on a sheepskin book cover.

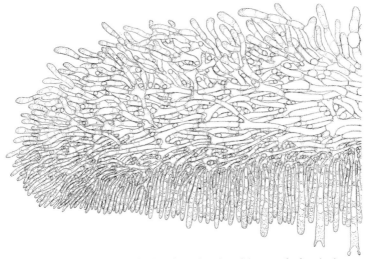

Magnified view of filamentous hyphae from the edge of the cap of a fruit body of the black trumpet mushroom, *Craterellus cornucopioides*.

sameness to mushroom anatomy that belies the complexity and reproducibility of the amazing range of fruit body shapes and sizes.

In 1718 the Florentine investigator Pier Antonio Micheli carried out the first experiments on mushroom development.[2] He began by placing fruit bodies of different species on heaps of fallen leaves with the purpose of inoculating the leaves with their 'seeds'. After a few hours he discarded the mushrooms and moved the leaves to shady locations. Visiting his compost after a spell of rainy weather, he observed the growth of 'white and thin down' on the edges of the decomposing leaves. A few weeks later he discovered fruit bodies of the same species that he had used at the start of the investigation. Mushroom cultivation on animal manure had been described a few years earlier, but Micheli's careful experiments verified the causal connection between successive generations of fruit bodies. He had disproved spontaneous generation more than a century before Louis Pasteur's much more famous rebuttal based on bacterial spoilage.

Micheli included details of his experiments in a book titled *Nova plantarum genera*, which described 1,900 species of plants and fungi.

Eighteenth-century illustration of the structure of earth-stars by Anton Micheli.
Note the expulsion of spores from the fruit body shown bottom right.

The spectacular plates in this work illustrate the anatomy of fruit
bodies and show how some species develop and release their spores.
Mushroom spores were illustrated as small groups of dots or as dust
expelled from puffballs and earth-stars. The microscopes available
to Micheli did not allow him to see in any greater detail.

Some of the Latin names for fungi proposed by Micheli are
still used today. These include *Aspergillus* (species of microscopic

Octopus stinkhorn, *Clathrus archeri.*

moulds), *Clathrus* (evil-smelling fungi related to stinkhorns), *Polyporus* (bracket fungi, or polypores) and *Tuber* (truffles). Other botanists described species of mushrooms in the eighteenth century, but experimental studies on fungi were not taken any further. Micheli was far ahead of his time and later investigators did not consider the microscopic features of the fungi they described; their approach to nature was wholly macroscopic. After Micheli's death in 1737, the Linnaean system of classification energized the study of plant taxonomy, but Linnaeus and his contemporaries were indifferent to the beauty of mushrooms. For reasons that defy my comprehension, they found flowering plants more interesting.

Mycology was rebooted in the nineteenth century and developed as a separate scientific endeavour rather than as a sideline of botany. Christiaan Hendrik Persoon and Elias Magnus Fries developed competing systems for classifying fungi, and experimental mycology was championed by Heinrich Anton de Bary. De Bary wrote the first textbook on fungi in the 1860s. This influential book described how major groups of fungi could be distinguished by their microscopic characteristics, introduced the biology of smut and rust fungi, which cause plant diseases, and explained how mushrooms were produced from colonies of branching hyphae that grow in soil and rotting wood. Other influential Victorian mycologists included the Reverend Miles Berkeley, who identified the microbial pathogen (not a fungus) that caused potato blight, and the Tulasne brothers, Charles and Louis-René (known as Edmond), who discovered that single species of fungi produce different growth forms. The Tulasnes' research was important because it highlighted the mistaken double naming of two stages in the development of a single fungus.

These advances in the study of fungi were made at the same time Pasteur was working on fermentation by yeast. Yeast research was viewed more as a part of microbiology, which progressed as a clinical field of science, than the concern of mycologists. Mycology lost some professional respect at this time through its miscasting as a subject reserved for naturalists who collected mushrooms. The assessment by microbiologists of a lot of mycology as observational in nature was fair, but taxonomists who scrutinized mushrooms were also learning a great deal about the structure and function of fruit bodies. Improvements in microscope design, for example, allowed them to discover the specialized cells called basidia that produced spores on the surfaces of mushroom gills. Micheli had glimpsed groupings of spores on gills a century earlier, but the dreadful optics furnished by his microscopes prevented him from seeing any details.

Another important advance in the nineteenth century was made by Julius Oscar Brefeld, who had been a student of de Bary. Brefeld developed methods for growing fungal colonies on gelatin free from bacteria and other microorganisms and was successful in raising fruit bodies of a little ink cap, *Coprinopsis stercorea*, from spores. This experimental work, based in Germany, continued through the twentieth century and provided the foundation for our understanding of mushroom biology.

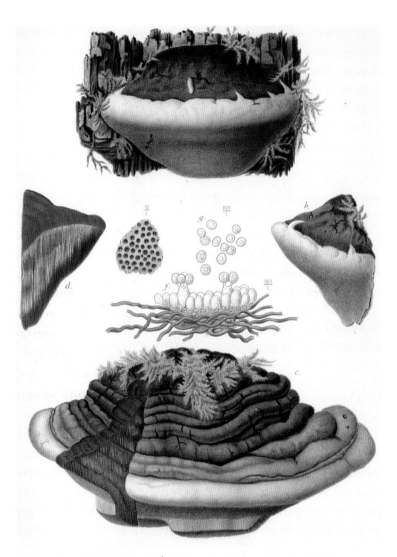

*Phellinus igniarius* by Jean-Louis Émile Boudier, illustrated in 1905. Basidia-producing basidiospores are shown in the highly magnified image in the centre of the illustration.

A. H. Reginald Buller (1874–1944), who spent his academic career at the University of Manitoba, is, without question, the most important mycologist in history. Buller studied many kinds of fungi, but his most important work was on the way that mushrooms release spores. He began by studying the shower of spores that falls from mushroom caps and watched clouds of these particles swirl away from the fruit body. The release of spores is made visible as a glittering dust by shining a lamp below a mushroom in the dark. Using a microscope, Buller counted the number of spores that dropped from a small section of gills and calculated that a mushroom could release thirty thousand spores per second. This means that even a short-lived fruit body can cast billions of spores into the air. Buller also looked at puffballs, and other kinds of mushrooms without gills, and calculated their astonishing spore output.

Almost nothing was known about the mechanism that launches spores from mushroom gills before Buller turned his attention to it. By combining meticulous observation with clever experiments, he made accurate predictions about the way the mechanism must work without any direct observation of the movement of the spores. Buller's work on spores was validated a century after his experiments, when high-speed video technology allowed investigators to observe the details of the discharge process.[3] Later in his career, Buller worked on the development of mushroom colonies and discovered a new reproductive process, known today as the 'Buller Phenomenon'. Other contributions to mycology included his measurements of the weight-lifting ability of expanding mushrooms, which allows them to burst through rotting wood and emerge from soil, experiments on bioluminescence, and the earliest description of programmed cell death (apoptosis), which Buller recognized in ink caps. His influence on the study of fungi is so important that he has been called 'the Einstein of mycology'. Buller published most of his experimental work in a seven-volume series of books, *Researches on Fungi*.[4] The *Researches* are the bible of mycology, the foundational documents of this field of study. Today's researchers in cell biology and genetics often begin their published papers by citing work from these volumes.

The British mycologist C. T. Ingold, who died in 2010, popularized Buller's experiments on spore discharge and inspired new generations of mycologists after the Second World War. Developments in instrumentation were critical to the next phase of mushroom science. New views of mushrooms came with the use of electron microscopes in the 1970s. The transmission electron microscope provided highly magnified images of thin tissue slices, and the scanning electron microscope showed the surface details of intact tissues. The combination of the two techniques provided mycologists with a more detailed picture of mushroom anatomy but did not answer fundamental questions about development. Part of the difficulty is evident in the earliest observations on mushroom structure made by Robert Hooke: everywhere we look inside a mushroom we see the same intermeshed filaments. The

Diagram showing the interior of a hyphal tip based on early studies using the transmission electron microscope.

organization of the filamentous hyphae is controlled by genetics and cannot be understood simply by looking at the structure of fruit bodies.

Genetic studies, beginning in the early twentieth century, showed how the formation of most species of mushrooms required the fusion of two colonies of different mating types. When molecular genetic techniques were introduced in the 1980s, investigators learned how specific genes controlled fungal reproduction. One of the surprises of these experiments was that some mushroom species existed in tens of thousands of different mating types. Mushroom gender and sexuality was more complicated than anyone had imagined. Analysis of mutant strains of mushrooms with misshapen fruit bodies provided clues about normal fruit body development, but we still have very little information about the way that a hypha in a mushroom stem is 'told' that it must grow long and thin, and how cells in the cap become reorganized at the gill surface to produce spores. The mysteries of fungal development can seem frustrating. One of the reasons for this lack of progress is that so few biologists study mushrooms. Problems in animal development have been solved by communities of thousands of scientists who have worked on model organisms like fruit-flies, roundworms and zebra fish. On the other hand, the fact that we know so little about something of such apparent simplicity as a mushroom can be a source of inspiration.[5]

Mushroom evolution has been explored with greater success using modern methods of molecular biology. This is the business of 'molecular phylogenetics'. Comparisons between the genes of mushrooms offer an objective guide to their ancestry. The genes in a fly agaric mushroom, *Amanita muscaria*, are more similar to the genes in a death cap, *Amanita phalloides*, than to the genes in a blewit, *Clitocybe* (or *Lepista*) *nuda*. Fly agaric and death cap are more closely related than either fungus is to the blewit. This conclusion rests on comparisons between particular genes that work as molecular clocks, changing at relatively slow rates as time passes. The affinity between the fly agaric and death cap is anticipated by the similarity in the general form of the mushroom. Both species have rings on their stems, white gills, white spores and the same overall shape. This is the reason that these fungi were assigned to the genus *Amanita* long before there was any understanding of evolution. The blewit looks very different. It has a lovely lilac colour, a bare stem and pink spores. A French botanist published the first description of the blewit in 1790.

If similarities in appearance always worked as an accurate indication of ancestry, we would not need to resort to molecular studies to organize the mushrooms into groups of related species. The identity of humans as a species of great ape is obvious to anyone looking into the eyes of a chimpanzee. But mushroom evolution has produced some surprising next of kin. When we compare the pair of *Amanita* species and the blewit with other mushrooms, we find that they have enough in common in terms of genetics to classify them in the order of fungi called the Agaricales. The surprise about the Agaricales is that in addition to incorporating most kinds of gilled mushroom, the group includes giant

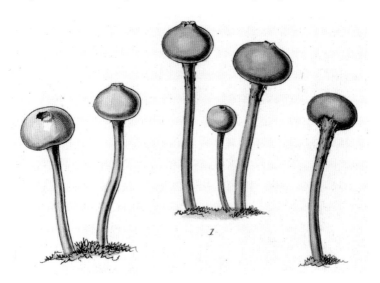

Stalked puffballs formed by a species of *Tulostoma*.

puffballs, stalked puffballs that grow in sandy soil (*Tulostoma* and *Podaxis*), blubbery bracket fungi (*Fistulina*) and beautiful coral fungi. Without genetic analysis there would be no way to craft a system of classification based on evolutionary relatedness, which is the primary mission of modern taxonomy. Understanding how puffballs evolved from gilled mushrooms is another matter, and the fossil record for fungi is too limited to offer a guide. We return to evolution in Chapter Four, after we have considered the diversity of the sixteen thousand living mushroom species.

*three*

# Mushroom Diversity

In the modern scheme of fungal classification, mycologists recognize more than twenty large groups, or taxonomic orders, of mushrooms. These incorporate gilled mushrooms and those with pores, species with spines that hang from their caps, chanterelles with ripples and folds rather than gills, bracket fungi, puffballs, bird's nest fungi, stinkhorns, jelly fungi, and far more besides than a sentence should contain. This assembly is joined with the rusts and smuts in the wider group or phylum of fungi called the Basidiomycota, or, less formally, the basidiomycetes. Rusts and smuts are parasites of plants, and do not produce fruit bodies like mushrooms. The stalked fruit bodies of morels and their relatives are also pictured in books and websites concerned with mushroom identification. These are ascomycete mushrooms belonging to the phylum Ascomycota, rather than basidiomycete mushrooms. Mushroom diversity is explored in this chapter by considering species from selected groups to illustrate the range of shapes, sizes and colours that can be found in forests and grasslands.

Beginning with the nineteenth-century schemes of fungal classification, naturalists organized mushrooms according to the presence of gills, pores or teeth beneath their caps. The colour of 'spore prints' that accumulate on a piece of paper placed under a mushroom cap was another guide used in earlier mycological studies. Genetic comparisons reveal the limitations of these observational methods of classification, but the identification of mushrooms in nature continues to rely on the recognition of visible characteristics. These more traditional skills in 'field mycology' are critical for anyone who collects mushrooms for cooking. Errors in mushroom identification can be lethal.

The order Agaricales encompasses most of the described mushroom species. The abbreviation 'agaric' used to be applied to any and every gilled mushroom. More recently, we have learned that many gilled mushrooms are unrelated and, unexpectedly, that many mushrooms without gills are genuine agarics. Gilled agarics include species of *Agaricus*, *Amanita*, *Cortinarius* and *Mycena*. The cultivated white button mushroom (*Agaricus bisporus*) and its wild relative, the field or meadow mushroom (*Agaricus campestris*), are among the best-known mushrooms in Europe and North America. A handful of other *Agaricus* species are described in guidebooks, but more than 250 species of *Agaricus* are described in the technical literature. Many of the more obscure mushroom species grow in tropical ecosystems and are seen by few people.

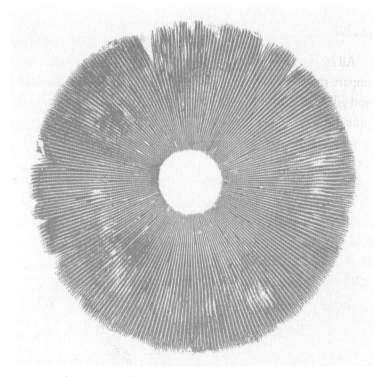

Spore print from the cap of a gilled mushroom.

Meadow mushroom, *Agaricus campestris.*

All of the *Agaricus* species have chocolate-brown spores that impart the same colour to the gills. This match between spore and gill colour is not evident in younger fruit bodies, which have pink gills. Another feature of many *Agaricus* species is a ring, or annulus, that is positioned towards the top of the stem. The ring develops as a membrane, called the partial veil, which covers the bottom of the gills in the unexpanded button or egg stage of the mushroom. As the fruit body inflates, the membrane is tugged away from the outer edge of the cap and tends to flop down around the stem. Rings are not present in all agarics, which makes them an important feature for mushroom identification.

Ringed stems are common among the six hundred described species of *Amanita*. A second membrane, or universal veil, surrounds the whole of the developing egg of *Amanita* species. This membrane is split into scales on the top of the cap as the mushroom expands and the lower portion remains as a cup, or volva, at the base of the stem. Some *Amanita* species have a ring on the stem,

Expansion of the death cap, *Amanita phalloides*.

scales on the cap and a cup at the base. Others feature one or two of these structures. Identification of these agarics is critical because they include delicious edibles, including Caesar's mushroom, *Amanita caesarea*, and *Amanita fulva*, the grisette, as well as the lethal death cap, *Amanita phalloides*, and destroying angel, *Amanita bisporigera*.

To paraphrase the geneticist J.B.S. Haldane, in the name of sexual equality and mycology, 'The Creator, if She exists, has an inordinate fondness for webcaps.' (Haldane suggested that 'He' fancied beetles.) *Cortinarius*, the webcap genus, comprises more than two thousand described species. Latin and common names for these fungi refer to the cobweb of strands (*cortina* is Late Latin for curtain) that is stretched across the bottom of the gills as the cap expands. This web is a version of the partial veil that remains as a ring on the stems of *Agaricus* and *Amanita* species. Webcaps, like *Amanita* species, are an advertisement for the importance of mushroom identification. Two webcaps, *Cortinarius rubellus* and *Cortinarius orellanus*, are very poisonous. Other webcaps are edible, including the gypsy mushroom, *Cortinarius caperatus*, which is enjoyed by wild mushroom enthusiasts in Europe.

Webcaps form 'mycorrhizal' partnerships with the roots of conifers and hardwood trees. *Amanita* species are also mycorrhizal and *Agaricus* contains a mixture of mycorrhizal and 'saprotrophic' mushrooms. The colonies of saprotrophic mushrooms decompose organic matter in soil and rotting wood. Colonies of *Mycena* feed as saprotrophs on wood and form clusters of fruit bodies on rotting logs. *Mycena* fruit bodies are no more than a few centimetres tall. They have conical or bell-shaped caps and their colours range from pure white to lilac, blue, yellow, brown, orange, pink and red. Most of the bioluminescent mushrooms are green-glowing *Mycena* species that grow in tropical forests.

Mushrooms produced by species of *Coprinus*, *Coprinopsis*, *Coprinellus* and *Parasola* are called ink caps. The caps of these saprotrophic fungi liquefy, or deliquesce, as they age, turning into inky black liquid at their edges and dripping onto the surrounding ground. By destroying the outer edges of the cap, these fruit bodies expose younger parts of the gill surfaces closer to the stem. This is thought to foster spore dispersal.

Web or cortina (right) stretched beneath the expanding cap of *Cortinarius trivialis*.

Gilled mushrooms produced by species outside the Agaricales include the fruit bodies of *Lactarius* and *Russula*, which are classified in the Russulales order. *Lactarius* and *Russula* are mycorrhizal fungi. *Lactarius* species are called milkcaps because they exude white latex when they are damaged. Mushroom gills provide a large surface area for spore release. The importance of gills is illustrated by the species of *Termitomyces* mushrooms farmed by termites in West Africa. These edible fungi fruit when the insects abandon their nests. Caps of *Termitomyces titanicus* can exceed a diameter of 1 metre. If the gills of these fruit bodies were flattened into a disc, the width of the cap would be 4.5 m, larger than a beach umbrella. Relative to a flattened disc, gills increase the surface area for spore release by a factor of twenty.[2] Comparable gains in surface area are made by mushrooms that develop tubes and teeth. Most of the Boletales and Polyporales release their spores from vertical tubes rather than gills. These tubes can extend for a centimetre or more through the flesh of the mushroom and end in a flat surface of pores on the underside of the cap. Mushroom spores, called basidiospores, are discharged from the inner surface of the tubes,

Shaggy ink cap, *Coprinus comatus*, with dripping gill edges.

*Termitomyces reticulatus* fruiting from a termite mound in Namibia.

drop through the centre of these thin cylinders and are swept away by air flowing around the cap when they emerge from the pores.

There are more 1,300 species of Boletales. These mycorrhizal fungi include a number of edible mushrooms, including *Boletus edulis*, known as porcini or cep. The brown cap has a convex shape in young mushrooms and flattens as the fruit body ages. The pores are very small, with two or three occupying each millimetre of the yellowish bottom of the cap. A hand lens is needed to see them properly. *Boletus edulis* has a similar shape to the poisonous Satan's bolete, *Boletus satanus*. Fortunately, it is impossible to mistake the two species: the cep has a brownish stem, whereas the stem of the Satan's bolete is a gorgeous red colour and turns blue where it is bruised. (Having said this, I diced a large Satan's bolete many years ago and added it to a stew because I did not take the time to consult a guide! The outcome would have been different if I had made the same mistake with a death cap.)

The Polyporales, or polypores, are wood-decay fungi and some species are parasites that attack living trees. Species whose fruit bodies jut horizontally from tree trunks are called shelf fungi or bracket fungi. These include *Ganoderma applanatum*, the artist's conk, and *Fomitopsis pinicola*, the red-belt conk. 'Conk' refers to the hard, woody texture of these fruit bodies. Fruit bodies of *Ganoderma lucidum*, the lingzhi or reishi mushroom, have been used in traditional Chinese medicine for two thousand years. Other medicinal mushrooms in the Polyporales include *Grifola frondosa*, maitake or hen-of-the-woods, and *Trametes versicolor*, the turkey tail. The striking orange and yellow sulphur shelf, *Laetiporus sulphureus*, also known as chicken-of-the-woods, is an edible polypore that is widely distributed. Wood-decay fungi whose fruit bodies develop as flattened crusts on the underside of logs and dead branches are related to these species. They are called corticioid fungi.

The table opposite lists groups of mushrooms with many different arrangements of tissues that produce spores. *Hydnum repandum* is a lovely white mushroom with spines under its cap. This is an edible species whose common name is the hedgehog mushroom. *Hydnum* is a member of the same group of fungi as another delicious mushroom, the golden chanterelle, *Cantharellus cibarius*. Chanterelles have thick folds beneath their caps. Spines and folds are alternative ways of shaping mushrooms that

Satan's bolete, *Boletus satanus*.

# Mushroom Taxonomy

Basidiomycete mushrooms divided into classes and orders

| CLASSES | EXAMPLES OF ORDERS | REPRESENTATIVE SPECIES |
|---|---|---|
| Agaricomycetes* | Agaricales | meadow mushroom, *Agaricus campestris* |
| | Boletales | cep or porcini, *Boletus edulis* |
| | Russulales | saffron milk cap, *Lactarius deliciosus* |
| | Polyporales | dryad's saddle, *Polyporus squamosus* |
| | Geastrales | earth-star, *Geastum triplex* |
| | Gomphales | club fungus, *Clavariadelphus pistillaris* |
| | Phallales | stinkhorn, *Phallus impudicus* |
| | Cantharellales | chanterelle, *Cantharellus cibarius* |
| | Auriculariales | Jew's ear, *Auricularia auricula-judae* |
| Dacrymycetes | Dacrymycetales** | jelly fungus, *Calocera cornea* |
| Tremellomycetes | Tremellales** | yellow witches' butter, *Tremella mesenterica* |

*More than twenty orders have been named in the Agaricomycetes. The orders not listed here include fungi that form brackets, crusts and truffle-like fruit bodies.

**Other orders in these classes do not form conspicuous fruit bodies.

Violet coral, *Clavaria zollingeri*.

Fruit bodies of the bird's nest fungus *Cyathus striatus*.

increase the surface area for spore release rather than making gills or tubes. These structures develop in many of the orders of mushroom-forming basidiomycetes. Coral fungi are equally scattered across the multitude of mushroom groups. These beautiful mushrooms release their spores from the exposed surface of their fruit bodies, which are variously shaped as simple spindles, forking staghorns and intricately branched candelabras.

The mechanism of basidiospore discharge is disrupted if water runs over the spores before release. Mushrooms with caps protect their gills from rain and avoid any interruptions to spore release. Spore release in the coral fungi is affected by a downpour and resumes when the storm passes. This problem is immaterial for puffballs because they have dispensed with the active mechanism of spore discharge. Spores of the common puffball, *Lycoperdon perlatum*, mature inside the fruit body and are expelled in an upward jet when the skin is compressed by raindrops. This fungus works rather like a nasal spray, although a spritz of irritating spores would have the opposite effect of a nasal decongestant. Giant puffballs of *Calvatia gigantea* can grow to a diameter of 1.5 m and weigh 20 kg. Fruit bodies of this size produce trillions of spores. Earthstars function in the same way as puffballs, but their bags of spores are cradled in an outer rind that peels open in the shape of a star. In one earth-star, called *Geastrum fornicatum*, the rind becomes inverted as it opens and acts as a platform that raises the bag a few millimetres above the ground. The spores of earth-balls are also dispersed when raindrops land on the fruit body. Earth-balls evolved from boletes. Fruit bodies of bird's nest fungi look like the nests of impossibly small birds. 'Eggs' of bird's nest fungi contain millions of spores and they are splashed from their nests by raindrops.

False truffles and stinkhorns rely on animals for dispersal. False truffles develop below ground and look like 'true' truffles that are formed by ascomycete fungi. They are unearthed and eaten by rodents, which disperse the spores in their faeces.

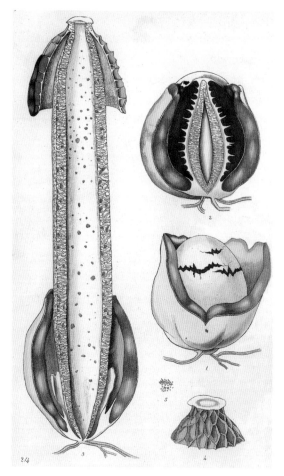

Anatomy of the common stinkhorn, *Phallus impudicus*, revealed by halving the mature fruit body and its egg stage.

Stinkhorn spores are dispersed by insects and slugs attracted to the odour of rotting flesh produced by the slimy mass of spores on the head of the mushroom. The common stinkhorn, *Phallus impudicus*, is related to seventy or more other mushroom species that attract insects to their spore slime. These mushrooms emerge from buried eggs; the tissues in the mature fruit body can be identified as layers in this 'embryo'. The artillery fungus, *Sphaerobolus stellatus*, which is related to earth-stars, uses its fruit body as a miniature cannon that propels a ball filled with spores into the air.

Mushrooms with a rubbery or gelatinous texture grow on rotting wood. These jelly fungi include the wood ear, *Auricularia auricula-judae*, which is common on elder; the yellow witches' butter, *Tremella mesenterica*; and the black witches' butter, or black jelly roll, *Exidia glandulosa*. Like the coral fungi, jelly fungi form basidiospores over their exposed surfaces. Spore formation is shut down when the fruit bodies dry out, but resumes within minutes after rehydration. In this fashion, jelly fungi release spores from their surfaces during an extended period of alternating wet and dry weather conditions.

Morels and false morels are ascomycete mushrooms. In place of a cap, these fungi have heads that are honeycombed, deeply ridged,

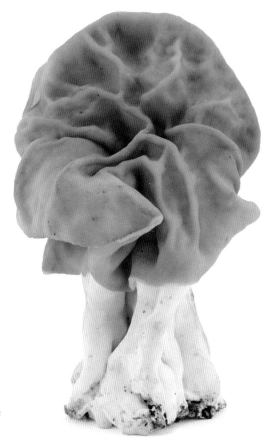

False morel, *Gyromitra esculenta.*

rippled or smooth. Ascomycete spores are discharged from cells called asci that operate like pressurized cannons. The ascospores are shot at very high speeds and travel much further than basidiospores. If asci developed on gills, the spores would be propelled from gill to gill and wasted in a pointless internal bombardment. This is avoided because morel asci are arranged on the surface of the mushroom head so that the spores are shot into the air directly. *Morchella esculenta*, the yellow morel, attracts American mushroomers in the spring and has become a familiar ingredient in wild mushroom recipes. It is less common in Europe, where it fruits in the early summer. False morels, which look like species of *Morchella*, include *Verpa bohemica* and *Gyromitra esculenta*. The convoluted brown head of a large specimen of *Gyromitra* looks like a human brain. Despite the name *esculenta*, which means edible, this fungus is highly toxic. The Latin name is endorsed, however, by fans of false morel consumption, who parboil the mushroom to remove the toxin before cooking the fungus in cream sauce. *Helvella crispa*, the elfin saddle, is another kind of ascomycete whose fruit body has a stem.

Some mushroom guides refer to an even broader range of ascomycetes as mushrooms, allowing any fungus with a fruit body that can be seen without a microscope to qualify. Whether or not we accept this liberal definition, the variety of mushrooms is staggering. Patience is required to learn the art and science of mushroom identification. Field mycologists spend a lifetime studying the assortment of species within a few hours' drive of their homes and experts have invested entire careers in exploring a single genus of mushrooms. Thanks to the modern molecular study of mushrooms, we have a clearer view of their genetic relationships than anyone imagined a few years ago, but a lot of fundamental questions about the nature of fungal species remain unanswered. In the next chapter we explore how this magnificent range of organisms evolved.

*four*
# Mushroom Evolution

The study of mushrooms began long before Charles Darwin took biology in a new direction with his insights on evolution. The first mycologists accepted the biblical account of Creation and were motivated to produce an ordered description of mushrooms that reflected the visible similarities and differences between fruit bodies. Through meticulous observation, these pioneers made remarkable strides in documenting mushroom diversity by arranging species into genera and slotting similar genera into larger groups. Zoologists approached animals in the same way, classifying humans as primates without any doubt that we were created separately from other animals and that we alone possessed souls.

Some of the early fungal taxonomy has survived the rigours of genetic analysis. Persoon and Fries named many mushrooms as species of *Amanita* because they shared white spores and some combination of scaly caps, ringed stems and cups at the base of their fruit bodies. In this case, similarities in appearance are a consequence of common ancestry and *Amanita* has endured as a 'reliable' genus for more than two hundred years. Other genera and larger groups of fungi based on the visible characteristics of the fruit body have been disbanded because this has proved an inaccurate guide to relatedness. Ancestry is the chief concern of the modern 'natural' classification of mushrooms. Beyond the scientific interest in questions of origins and relationships, this area of study has practical value. Related mushrooms tend to produce similar kinds of toxins and other bioactive molecules. This means that a natural classification can be helpful in the search for pharmacological agents. If, for example, a compound with antibiotic activity is isolated from a bolete, it may be worthwhile these remarkable discoveries, mushroom fossils are very scarce and offer no clues to the ways that fruit bodies have changed over time. To learn about the evolutionary history of mushrooms we rely upon genetic comparisons between living species. Genetic studies do not necessarily point to the first mushrooms, only to the oldest groups that have survived. They suggest that some of the jelly fungi are really ancient, with a history that stretches back to the end of the Carboniferous period. The wood ear mushroom, *Auricularia auricula-judae*, is a modern representative of these primeval mushrooms.[2] The brown fruit bodies of *A. auricula-judae* are usually a few centimetres in width and exceptional specimens grow to the size of a mobile phone. The Latin name *Auricularia* refers to ears, but ears are too thick for perfect comparison. When they are fully hydrated they feel a little like human *labia minora*. The name of the species is translated to Jew's ear, which refers to Judas, who hanged himself from an elder tree as penance for his sin. Elder is one of the plants that this fungus decomposes. The biblical reference and unintentional anti-Semitism are avoided in guides, which

*Pseudohydnum gelatinosum*, a beautiful toothed jelly fungus.

John Augustus Knapp's painting of golden chanterelles, *Cantharellus cibarius*, commissioned by the mycologist Curtis Gates Lloyd.

shorten the name to *Auricularia auricula*. The gelatinous texture of the wood ear comes from the production of masses of mucilage by the filaments within the fruit body. Jelly fungus spores develop on the surface of the fruit body, are discharged into the air and swept away by air currents. The wood ear is a far simpler structure than the agarics that evolved much later. It is a mycological coelacanth, or living fossil. *Pseudohydnum gelatinosum* is a related jelly fungus that produces a stalked fruit body with teeth under its slimy

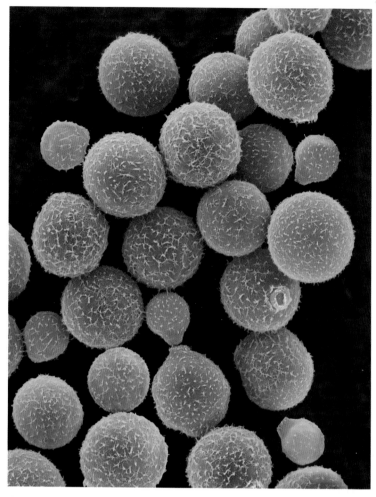

Scanning electron micrograph of group of dividing cells of *Cryptococcus neoformans*.

modifications in spore-release mechanism. The mature meadow mushroom has gills and the puffball is a loose bag. Small mushrooms tend to release fewer spores than do large mushrooms, but a fungus that produces many tiny fruit bodies can shed just as many spores as the colony of second species that forms one or two large mushrooms. Other distinctions cannot be explained so easily. We do not understand why some fruit bodies have flattened caps and others are more rounded. Cap shape affects

The psychotropic liberty cap, *Psilocybe semilanceata*, whose fruit bodies have conical caps.

airflow and spore dispersal, but subtle variations in shape may not serve a particular function.[4] The presence of an umbo, or nipple, on the top of the hallucinogenic liberty cap, *Psilocybe semilanceata*, is a good example of an interesting shape that has no apparent influence on the operation of the fruit body. Characteristics of this sort may exist for the simple reason that they are not associated with any reduction in spore release and the formation of new colonies. Natural selection has not had the opportunity to say no to liberty cap nipples and so they are here to stay.

Mushroom colour is a puzzle too. *Russula virescens* produces a green cap; caps of *Russula emetica* are painted the same red as old British telephone boxes. The significance of being a green *Russula* rather than a red *Russula*, or a *Russula* species that blackens when bruised, is a mystery. We know that the colours of flower petals are matched to their attractiveness to pollinating insects, but we have no comparable explanation for the colour palette of mushrooms. Mushroom fragrance is another phenomenon whose function is obscure. We tend to assume that an ornamental shape, painted cap and the release of odour affects the way a fungus works, because these modifications require an energy investment by the fungus. This is a topic that deserves more attention from researchers.

There is, then, no simple explanation for the diversity of mushrooms. The facade of the fruit body is obviously very malleable and can be altered in many ways to accommodate different mechanisms of spore release. Mushrooms are like insects in this respect. Insect bodies and mushrooms can be enlarged or reduced, stretched one way and condensed in another, ornamented and re-coloured without disrupting their life cycles. Changes of this sort have occurred in fungal populations over millions of years with the appearance of new ecological opportunities, resulting in the marvellous variety of mushrooms that we find in the woods.

# *five*
# Mushroom Sexuality

The resemblance of some fruit bodies to human genitalia is explained by the necessities of thrusting through compacted soil (which gives many emerging mushrooms a somewhat phallic appearance), displaying a head of spore slime to attract insects (augmenting the phallic shape of stinkhorns), and becoming slippery with mucilage to maintain hydration after rainfall (in the more labial-looking jelly fungi). While these similarities are apparent to everyone, the nature of mushrooms as sexual organisms that reproduce after mating requires an imaginative stretch on the part of most readers. This is because mating between the fungi that form mushrooms occurs in soil or rotting wood and is invisible without a microscope.

Colonies of branching filaments growing in a fallen tree feed by secreting digestive enzymes that release sugars and other small molecules from the dead wood. The sugars fuel the metabolism of the colony, allowing it to expand into all the available food. Mushroom colonies grow in soil according to the same mechanism, releasing enzymes to decompose plant roots and other materials. As the colony increases in size it may have the opportunity to merge with another colony and collaborate in the formation of mushrooms. For colonies growing on a small leaf pile, mushroom production and spore release are essential if the fungi – or, rather, the genes carried by these fungi – are going to survive. If a colony fails to reproduce, it will die when the nutrients in the leaves are exhausted.

Mushroom colonies, or mycelia, growing over much larger areas can persist for long periods of time. A celebrated colony of a honey fungus, *Armillaria solidipes*, spreads over 10 square km in

Oregon and has an estimated weight of 35,000 tons.[1] This giant mycelium has spread through forest soil, attacking conifers for 2,400 years, and is considered the world's largest organism. The Oregon honey fungus produces mushrooms and disperses spores, so it is on the move, but the parent mycelium will remain in the same location and keep growing as long as it finds food.

Before we look at the mating process, it is useful to consider the nature of the individual fungus. A single colony is an example of an individual. The question of identity is complicated by the observation that separate colonies can contain identical sets of genes. These identical individuals are clones. If one colony of a clone dies, its complete set of genes – its genome – is conserved in other clones. Human clones, or identical twins, exist as individuals

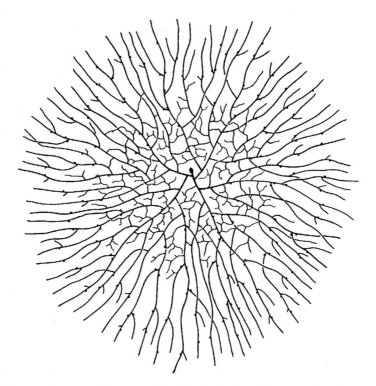

Diagram of a young colony or mycelium that has developed from a single mushroom spore at the centre.

in the same way. Sexual reproduction is the only way that a human genome can be transmitted from one generation to the next. Fungi have the option of reproducing without mating. This is called asexual reproduction. Mushroom mycelia can produce asexual spores without producing any fruit bodies, but sexual reproduction via mushrooms has a number of advantages. Sex is crucial for fungi because it allows parent colonies to produce offspring that carry new arrangements of genes. Some of these versions of the genome prosper because they increase the fitness of the colonies that contain them and this means that they are more likely to be replicated in later generations. Mushroom formation has the added bonus of allowing two colonies to combine resources and release lots of spores into the air.

Mating in mushrooms is determined by physical proximity and genetic compatibility. Growing in the same place is essential for an organism whose movement in soil is limited to the expansion of its mycelium. Hyphae extend at a top speed of 2 mm per day, which means that a pair of colonies separated by the width of this page will take more than a month to make contact. When, at last, the hyphae of two colonies of the same mushroom species touch, some individuals couple and merge the contents of their cells and others respond to the encounter by releasing toxins. Genes control whether colonies antagonize one another or make mushrooms. In the simplest version of this reproductive system, mating is managed by a single gene. As long as colonies carry different versions of this gene, they can unite and produce fruit bodies. The shaggy mane or lawyer's wig mushroom, *Coprinus comatus*, works in this way. Lawyer's wig is a large, edible, ink cap mushroom that is common on lawns. Other mushrooms have a more complicated method of copulating that involves multiple versions of a pair of genes. Mating between colonies of this kind is sanctioned as long as they carry different versions of both genes. Another ink cap mushroom, *Coprinopsis cinerea*, uses this mechanism.[2]

*Coprinopsis cinerea* fruiting in a Petri dish.

Mushroom mating types are identified as $A_1B_1$, $A_2B_3$, $A_4B_4$, and so on, rather than male and female, but we can think of them as different genders. Genetic analysis of populations of *Coprinopsis cinerea* shows that there are tens of thousands of mating types or sexes of this species and almost all of them are compatible. The evolution of this unusual mating system makes sense for an organism that has trouble finding a partner. An ink cap mycelium growing in soil is surrounded by bacteria and other fungi, but needs to make use of every chance encounter with a mycelium of its own kind if it is going to make mushrooms and disperse spores. If ink cap mycelia existed as males and females, half of all rendezvouses would not work. The proliferation of mating types permits the greatest variety of sexual liaisons between mycelia without allowing the closest relatives to mate with each another.

The fusion of mycelia is comparable with the first stage in the animal process of fertilization, when a sperm cell penetrates an egg. Fertilization is completed when the nucleus that carries the chromosomes in the sperm fuses with the nucleus in the egg. Something different takes place in mushrooms. Nuclei of the two mating types flow into the shared cell contents, but they remain separate until the fruit body develops and spores are formed. The mycelium is organized as a series of cell compartments separated by walls that cross the filamentous hyphae. After mating, the mycelium forms little branches on the surface of the hyphae called clamp connections. These serve as channels that distribute the nuclei so that one nucleus of each mating type is housed in every

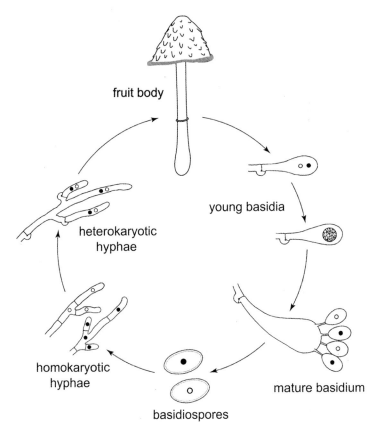

fruit body

young basidia

heterokaryotic hyphae

homokaryotic hyphae

basidiospores

mature basidium

Diagram of a mushroom life cycle. The technical terms 'homokaryotic' and 'heterokaryotic' refer, respectively, to the mushroom mycelium before and after mating. Clamp connections are visible as bumps on the surface of the hyphae following mating.

Fruit body bursting through asphalt paving.

cell compartment. Mycelia with this structure continue to feed and expand before they begin to form fruit bodies. Fungi are the only organisms that reproduce in this fashion.

Fruit body development is one of the seemingly miraculous processes that make fungi so fascinating. The appearance of a ring of mushrooms in the morning when nothing was visible in the same spot the previous evening is bound to attract attention. Nothing else in nature performs any comparable feat. Mushrooms expand so quickly because they are inflated by the absorption of water. In most species, this hydraulic process is accompanied by the rapid growth and branching of hyphae in the stem and cap of the mushroom. Before the fruit body is visible above ground, it exists as a primordium that ranges in size from that of a pea to that of a hen's egg. These embryonic mushrooms develop at different locations on the mycelium and draw upon the masses of materials accumulated by the feeding colony. Many of the details of this complex mechanism are not understood.

The biomechanics of mushroom emergence have been studied in detail. As the elongating stem absorbs water it becomes pressurized to the same level as a bicycle tyre and the cap is pushed upwards with a force capable of cracking asphalt on a driveway. The great Reggie Buller determined the weight-lifting ability of mushrooms in the 1930s by seeing how much lead shot developing fruit bodies could raise. Force measurements with a strain gauge made seventy years after Buller's experiments showed that the force exerted by mushrooms increases in a series of pulses.[3] Fruit bodies seem to work a bit like pneumatic drills, pushing then relaxing, pushing then relaxing. This behaviour is critical in enabling the mushroom to escape from the ground and expand its cap in the air.

The gills are exposed as the cap swells and spores are released in their billions. The millions of hyphae that form the mushroom run through its stem, outwards into the cap and end at the gill surfaces. Some of the hyphal tips are transformed into specialized cells called basidia that produce spores. Others pack around the basidia and have elaborate shapes, including spiked tips, whose functions are not understood. Basidia are cells at the ends of hyphae whose compartments contain one nucleus from each of the original mycelial partners that mated in the soil. These nuclei can be paired for months or even years after mating in the colony but they do not fuse until they are brought together in the basidia. This is the final step in fertilization. It is followed by the duplication and division of the DNA in the combined nucleus and the assortment of four complete sets of chromosomes into four nuclei. Each nucleus is packaged in a single spore and each basidium produces four spores. The spores are propelled from the gills, fall through the spaces between the gills, and are swept away by wind. When a spore lands on moist soil or rotting timber, it germinates to produce a new mycelium. This completes the wheel of life for a mushroom.

To summarize: fungi that form mushrooms reproduce sexually through the fusion of colonies of filamentous cells, followed by the formation of multicellular fruit bodies and release of spores that form new generations of colonies. This mechanism operates in most mushroom species, although details vary considerably. The basidia of jelly fungi, for example, look quite different from the basidia of gilled mushrooms, but they all produce spores after the combination of the nuclei of the two mating types. Some basidia produce two spores rather than four and others produce more than four spores. A few mushrooms are self-fertile, capable of producing fruit bodies and spores without mating at all. The cultivated button mushroom, *Agaricus bisporus*, is an example of a self-fertile mushroom and it produces only two spores per basidium.

Pier Antonio Micheli, the Florentine naturalist, provided the first illustrations of mushroom spores arranged in groups of four on the surface of gills. When his work was published in the eighteenth century, some authors continued to dispute the nature of fungi as living organisms. More enlightened botanists regarded fungi as primitive plants and Micheli thought that mushrooms produced miniature flowers. Micheli's observations on spores were ignored for almost a century and investigators published drawings of cell structures that are never seen on gills. This misapprehension seems to have been driven by the expectation of the types of cells that they thought they would find in mushrooms. It was, however, a surprising error in mycological history because basidia can be seen quite easily with a low-power microscope.

Worthington G. Smith was the uncontested master of delusional studies on mushrooms in the nineteenth century. In a pair of articles, he reported that 'long and patient observation' allowed him to see mushroom spores being fertilized by swimming sperm cells. This supposedly happened after the spores and other cells containing sperm were shed from the gills. He probably mistook other microorganisms in his microscopic samples for sperm cells, but this was definitely a low point in mycological research. He made other mistakes in his research, too, and poisoned himself and his family through an error in mushroom identification. The Smiths survived this blunder and, three years later, Worthington published an authoritative guide to distinguishing between edible and poisonous fungi. (I make no claim of superiority with respect to poisoning, having been lucky following my reckless consumption of an unfamiliar mushroom, as described in Chapter Three.) An accurate picture of mushroom sexuality, including the way that genes controlled mating types, emerged in the twentieth century. Some of the early work that illuminated the mating process was published by a 23-year-old Oxford graduate, Elsie Maud Wakefield, who went on to serve as the head of mycology at Kew for forty years.[4]

When we look at mushrooms in the woods, it is easy to forget that the fruit body is connected to a larger, invisible mycelium. By recognizing that a fruit body is one stage in a continuing cycle of life for a microorganism that lives below ground, we approach a richer appreciation of the whole fungus. This is important for anyone wanting to understand wider issues in mushroom biology, including ecology and conservation. Sex in mushrooms seems complicated because it is so different from the familiar fertilization of eggs by motile sperm in animals. The effectiveness of the unique mushroom version of sexual reproduction is evident in the diversity and long evolutionary history of these fungi.

*six*

# Mushroom Function

Spore release is the reason for being a mushroom. Basidiomycete fungi make a huge investment when they move resources from the buried mycelium into their fruit bodies. Through this process, the *microscopic* feeding phase of the life cycle is replaced with *macroscopic* reproductive organs that produce staggering numbers of spores. A single meadow mushroom, *Agaricus campestris*, releasing tens of thousands of spores per second, will shed ten billion spores in four days. Trillions of spores can be scattered from a single dried sack of the related giant puffball, *Calvatia gigantea*. Other less conspicuous fungi match the spore output of larger mushrooms by producing lots of tiny fruit bodies. A cluster of three hundred fairy ink caps, produced by *Coprinellus disseminatus*, each with a cap diameter of 5 mm, matches the gill area of a solitary death cap mushroom, *Amanita phalloides*, with a 9 cm cap.[1] Fruiting more than once a year is another way to amplify spore production.

Fungi produce lots of spores for the same reason that fish like salmon produce so many fry: most offspring die. The odds that any single spore will land in a place where it can germinate, form a colony and mate with another mycelium before it is scorched by the sun or eaten by a worm are very small. One in a billion, which is a considerably lower probability than winning a lottery, is as good as it gets for a spore. The importance of dispersal has placed a premium upon the evolution of effective ways to release spores from fruit bodies. Mushrooms with gills, tubes (pores), spines, rippled and smooth surfaces, as well as coral and jelly fungi, use the same mechanism of active 'ballistospore' discharge. An understanding of this marvel of evolutionary engineering allows us to make sense of many of the facets of mushroom structure and diversity described in the previous chapters.

Mushroom spores develop from the cells called basidia that project from the gill surface. Each basidium looks like a four-pronged crown or a miniature cow udder. The tips of these prongs swell to form spores. When the spores reach full size, they sit on their prongs, primed for launch into the gill spaces. Water evaporates from the gills, cooling their surface and making the air in the gill spaces very humid. These conditions are perfect for spore release. A simple mechanism that allowed the spores to drop from their basidia would not be effective because spores would become stuck on basidia projecting from the gill surfaces below them. A powerful spurt mechanism would also fail by blasting the spores onto the opposite gill. The only solution to this mechanical problem is to launch the spores into the middle of the gaps between gills, so that they can fall freely from the fruit body. For 'poroid' mushrooms, the spores must be discharged into the centre of the tubes for successful release. Mature spores

Cluster of fairy ink caps, *Coprinellus disseminatus.*

Scanning electron micrograph of basidia bearing basidiospores on the gill surface of a grey shag, *Coprinopsis cinerea*.

maintain a very weak connection to their prongs. The mechanism of ballistospore discharge allows the spores to break contact with the basidia and jump between the gills. The description of spore discharge as a 'jump' is appropriate because it is similar to the physics of a standing jump. To jump, we bend our knees and then straighten our legs quickly, propelling ourselves into the air. Jumping allows us to leave the ground by shifting our centre of mass upwards, imparting momentum to the body. The mushroom spore achieves a similar displacement of mass via the rapid movement of a drop of fluid over its surface.[2]

It happens like this. In the seconds before each spore is released, a drop of fluid grows on the base of the spore. This is called 'Buller's drop'. At the same time, a second drop of water grows on the spore surface next to the first. When the two drops get big enough to touch one another, they slap together. The rapid movement of Buller's drop achieves the rapid shift in mass that catapults the spore from the gill. The movement of Buller's drop and the launch of the spore occur within a few millionths of a second. This process was not seen until 2005 when it was 'slowed down' using a high-speed video camera attached to a microscope. The video footage, captured at a camera speed of 100,000 frames per second, revealed the movement of the drop and almost instantaneous leap of the spore.[3] The launch speed of one metre per second is comparable to a flea's jump, but the spore accelerates much faster than the insect. The entire process, from the swelling of the young spores to spore discharge, can be completed in less than thirty minutes. It happens continuously over the gill surfaces – spores jumping every second from each patch of the gills – to support the blizzard of spores that pours from the cap.

Inspection of the surface architecture of a spore shows the locations where the fluid drops grow. The drops originate from water vapour in the humid air trapped between the gills. This vapour condenses into liquid water when it comes into contact with sugary molecules on the spore surface. The way that this is synchronized with the loosening of the connection between the spore and its basidium is a mystery. If the drops develop before the connection is weakened, the motion of Buller's drop

Magnified view of the underside of a mushroom cap showing tightly packed mushroom gills with intervening air spaces. Spores would be wasted if they were propelled onto the surface of the opposing gill, which explains why discharge distance is critical.

is not sufficient to power lift-off. Yet mature spores do sever their connections with the basidia a few seconds before the drops begin to expand, and, like clockwork, the drops slap together and thousands of spores jump from the gills in a flawless ballet.

Another subject of continuing inquiry is the way in which the ballistospore mechanism is fine-tuned in the thousands of mushroom species.[4] Some spores are discharged over much longer distances than others and large spores tend to jump further than small spores. Some of the largest spores are shot from mushrooms with thick, wide-spaced gills, like the rooting shank, *Xerula radicata*. Big spores are also formed by *Aleurodiscus oakesii* and its relatives, which grow as flat crusts on tree bark.

The precise length of the spore jump is very critical for boletes and other poroid fungi that release their spores from long and very narrow tubes. This mechanical challenge is particularly acute in brackets of the artist's fungus, *Ganoderma applantum*, whose tubes can be 2 cm long and a little wider than one-tenth of a millimetre. Spores must be shot into the dead centre of the tubes in order to fall to the openings on the underside of the bracket and escape into the surrounding air. Vertical positioning of the tubes is crucial and this is achieved by an undiscovered mechanism of gravitational sensing. We can see that this works by looking at a bracket that continues to grow on a log after a tree has fallen over. The tubes

Mechanism of basidiospore discharge involving the formation of two droplets of fluid (in blue) on the spore surface, and their coalescence that causes a redistribution of mass.

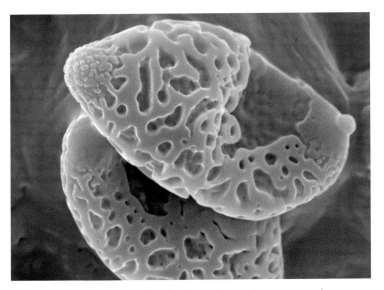

Scanning electron micrograph showing the intricate surface structure of a basidiospore of *Austroboletus mutabilis.*

that develop after the tree collapses grow at a different angle to ensure that they keep pointing towards the ground. Mushroom gills respond to gravity in the same way, growing downwards in perfect vertical orientation to promote spore release.

Mushrooms show many other adaptations that optimize the dispersal of spores. The evaporation of water from the fruit body chills the gills by a few degrees and this cooling is thought to stimulate the condensation of water on the spore surface. This cooling phenomenon is palpable in large mushrooms, whose caps can feel quite frigid to the touch on a warm day.[5] It has also been suggested that the evaporation of water creates airflow patterns that help to carry spores away from the fruit body.[6] Some studies have shown that a high proportion of mushroom spores fall quite close to the fruit body. This limits the exploration of new territory by the fungus and is a particular problem for fruit bodies growing in places where they are not exposed to wind.

Fungus gnats and other insects that visit fruit bodies carry spores on their hairy bodies and in their guts after feeding on

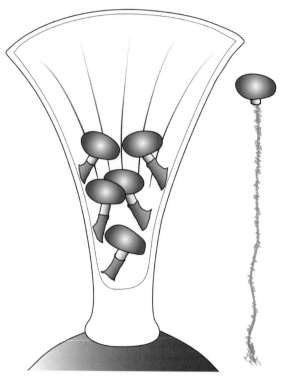

Fruit body structure in the bird's nest fungus *Cyathus striatus*. The dragline of the peridiole pictured outside the fruit body has been unravelled to its full length.

mushroom tissues. Larvae of species that lay their eggs in mushrooms may also disperse spores when they leave as adults. If insects are significant vectors for spore dispersal it seems likely that evolution has equipped fungi with some features that the couriers find attractive. The strongest evidence for this kind of adaptation has been found in a mushroom called *Neonothopanus gardneri*, which lures insects at night by emitting green light.[7] This mechanism was explored by using acrylic models of fruit bodies illuminated with green light-emitting diodes, to fool insects. *Neonothopanus* mushrooms grow at the base of palm trees in Brazilian forests, where they are sheltered from wind. It is not known whether insect attraction is connected with bioluminescence in other mushrooms.

The loss of the mechanism of active ballistospore discharge in puffballs, earth-stars and earth-balls is coupled with the use of raindrops to move spores; stinkhorns, false truffles and bird's nest fungi rely on animals for dispersal. Dispersal in puffballs and stinkhorns was described earlier in this book, but the complexity of the bird's nest fungi requires some deeper investigation. *Cyathus striatus* is a bird's nest fungus with a very complicated anatomy. It forms cups shaped like trumpets that hold up to twenty packets of spores called peridioles. Each peridiole contains two million spores, so a single fruit body with twenty of

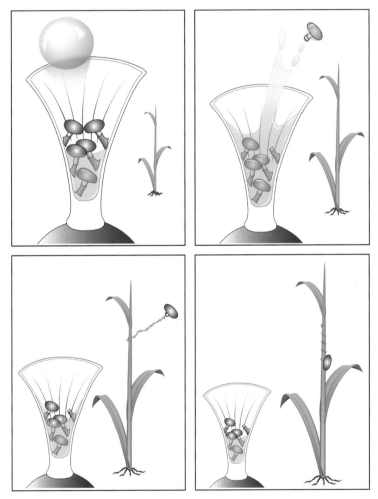

Splash discharge mechanism in the bird's nest fungus *Cyathus striatus*.

Group of four fruit bodies of the artillery fungus, *Sphaerobolus stellatus*, each with its single projectile filled with spores sitting in the centre of the glistening star-shaped cup.

them can release forty million spores. This is quite a modest number compared with the output from a gilled mushroom, but the reproductive strategy of the bird's nest fungus is completely different. Rather than releasing individual spores and betting that a small number will settle in a good place to begin a colony, the bird's nest fungus invests its energy in maximizing the chance that whole peridioles will be eaten by animals.

The mechanism is fascinating.[8] Each peridiole is equipped with a dragline that is folded inside a purse attached to its surface. When the peridiole is splashed from its nest by a raindrop, it flies through the air until it collides with an obstacle like a plant stem or lands on the ground. Collision with a plant is the preferred outcome for the fungus and this is the reason for having a dragline. When a peridiole hits a plant, the sticky end of the dragline at the opening of the purse fastens to the obstacle and the line unravels as the peridiole continues its short flight. When the dragline is fully extended, it jerks the peridiole back towards the plant, rather like a bungee cord. The peridiole then rotates around the plant stem until the dragline is wound up and rests against the stem. If the peridiole did not have a dragline, it would bounce off the plant rather than sticking to its surface.

This marvellous mechanism places the spores of the bird's nest fungus in the best location to be eaten by a browsing herbivore. Dispersal is assured by the passage of the peridiole through the digestive system of the animal and the deposition of the spores in its dung. The dung provides the germinating spores with moisture and a rich source of nutrients. Peridioles that are splashed onto the ground also seem to do well, and bird's nest fungi often grow on rotting wood. Without passage through an animal, however, the distribution of the spores is very limited. Molecular studies suggest that the bird's nest fungus evolved from a mushroom ancestor with gills. This must have involved the loss of the active mechanism of spore discharge, and the packaging of spores in peridioles, by way of an intermediate series of fungi that might have looked like puffballs.

The artillery fungus, *Sphaerobolus stellatus*, is another mushroom with a complex evolutionary history. This is more closely related to earth-stars than gilled mushrooms and has perfected a unique type of dispersal mechanism. Its unopened fruit bodies are white spheres with a diameter of 2 mm. They are easily overlooked, but can be found under shrubs after heavy rainfall, when they appear as patches of white dots. When each fruit body hatches, it opens in the shape of a star and cradles a single ball of spores in the middle of a glistening cup. The open fruit body works as a miniature mortar that flings the ball into the air when the inner layer of the cup flips outwards. The maximum range of the artillery fungus is 6 m, which is the longest of any mechanism of spore discharge in fungi. If the sticky ball lands on vegetation it may be eaten by herbivores and dispersed like the bird's nest fungus. The displacement of air caused by the explosive discharge of the artillery fungus is audible as a pop. This is the only sound made by a fungus that we can hear.

*seven*

# Mushroom Experts

The extraordinary contributions of A. H. Reginald Buller to our understanding of fungi are mentioned throughout this book. Part of the rationale for recognizing Buller as the Einstein of mycology comes from the manner in which he reached many of his conclusions before they could be proved by advances in microscopy and genetics. In similar fashion, Albert Einstein's genius is highlighted every time astrophysicists develop new ways to test the theory of general relativity. Before they picked up this book, some readers are likely to have laboured under the impression that elucidating the space-time continuum was more important than understanding spore release in mushrooms. With this view corrected, they may be interested in Buller's synopsis of relativity in a limerick published in *Punch* in 1923:

> There was a young lady named Bright,
> Whose speed was far faster than light;
> She started one day
> In a relative way,
> And returned on the previous night.

This was the high point of Buller's poetry, which otherwise dealt with issues of mycology. One autobiographical and dreadful verse titled 'The Sporobolomycetologist' concerned a mycologist who studied a yeast called *Sporobolomyces*. Buller's eccentricities were highly developed.

Reginald Buller was born in Birmingham and obtained his PhD from the University of Leipzig. His move to the University of Manitoba in 1904 allowed him to pursue an academic career

A.H.R. Buller,
the Einstein of
mycology.

free from the frustrations of the class system associated with work in the older British universities before the First World War. Another advantage of life on the wind-blown Canadian prairies was relief from the asthma that had plagued him in England. Buller had many women friends, but did not marry, expressing contentment with a life spent in greatest intimacy with his research and writing. He lived in hotels in Winnipeg throughout his career, with a stay of almost thirty years in one quite drab establishment called the McClaren.[1]

The study of mushrooms remained a descriptive enterprise for most mycologists in the early twentieth century. Buller's studies in Leipzig showed him the power of experimental work and he recognized that the field of mycology was ripe for discoveries. (Elsie Wakefield, a contemporary who adopted experimental approaches to her studies on mushrooms, also trained in Germany.) Buller's commitment to objective investigation became legendary. During experiments on bioluminescent mushrooms, he prepared for his early-morning commute from the McClaren Hotel to the university campus by strapping horse blinders to his head. This accoutrement helped preserve his night vision from the gas lighting in the city so that he could see the dim glow from the fruit bodies when he got to the laboratory. One can imagine the effect of this performance on fellow commuters who passed him on foot or saw him from the window of a streetcar.

Buller's exploits became legendary among his colleagues and students. The provenance of a second story is unreliable, but it sounds right. (I heard it second-hand from a retired colleague in Canada.) On a fungal foray north of Winnipeg, Buller was standing in his moth-eaten overcoat, lecturing about mushrooms. Distracted by a sudden shadow, he glanced towards the

Captain Charles McIlvaine, author of *One Thousand American Fungi* (1900).

sun, then cried out as an eagle latched its talons onto his bald head, screeched and flew away. Reggie was left with blood running down his face, stunned, swaying among the gathering of astonished students. Life for most of us is peppered with moments of stark humiliation, but few have been molested by an eagle.

In this brief discourse on scientific personalities, rather than science, two figures from the history of mycology in the United States demand attention: Captain Charles McIlvaine (1840–1909) and Curtis Gates Lloyd (1859–1926). McIlvaine was a veteran of the American Civil War who experienced a moment of revelation on horseback in the woods of West Virginia:'I saw on every side luxuriant growths of fungi, so inviting in color, cleanliness and flesh that it occurred to me they ought to be eaten.'[2] At a time of extreme rural poverty, McIlvaine believed he had discovered an abundance of food for free. The calorific value of fruit bodies is comparable to lettuce, making them better for weight loss than weight gain. Their value lies rather in their capacity to transform a bland staple, like boiled beans or grain, into a feast, and therein lay the value of the captain's investigations. McIlvaine set about testing the edibility of almost every mushroom he found in the forest and gathered his discoveries in a giant book entitled *One Thousand American Fungi*, which was published in 1900.

For each entry, McIlvaine provided a technical description of the species for the purpose of identification, and a record of its edibility. The bioluminescent mushroom *Panellus stipticus* did not delight the captain:'The immediate and lasting unpleasantness of this fungus, whether cooked or raw, will cancel all desire to eat of it forevermore ... No one but a determined suicide would resort to it.' A close relative of this mushroom that grows as a little fleshy bracket on trees, fared better:'Long, slow cooking makes it tender. It makes a luscious gravy after thirty minutes' stewing.' In many of the entries, McIlvaine enchanted his readers with comments on the beauty of his mushrooms. For a species of *Panus* he wrote: 'The markings upon the white margin are more precise than those of the finest bee comb. One does not tire looking at the work of Nature's geometrician.'

*One Thousand American Fungi* is not to be trusted as an authoritative guide to mushroom safety. The sulphur tuft, *Hypholoma fasciculare*, contains toxins that can cause vomiting, diarrhoea and convulsions. Yet McIlvaine wrote: 'wherever and however they grow, Hypholomas are safe. I have eaten them indiscriminately since 1881.' The toxicity of this mushroom seems to vary from place to place, and the captain may have inactivated the active chemicals by cooking, but he was playing with fire. There were, however, limits to his brashness and he warned his readers about the death cap, destroying angel and other dangerous species of *Amanita*. His selflessness as a test subject for toxicology, his love of whisky and military service combined in his nickname, 'Old Ironguts'.

Curtis Lloyd was more interested in naming mushrooms than eating them.[3] He objected, however, to the established method that appended the name of the author to the Latin name of new species. In his opinion, this encouraged narcissists to name lots of new 'species' based on trivial differences between varieties of the same mushroom. Lloyd was enthusiastic about collecting and describing new species himself, but did not want his name to come after the fungus. If I were to find a new species of mushroom with a black cap and name it *Agaricus nigra*, this would appear in future lists of species as *Agaricus nigra* Money. Lloyd would have preferred that the 'Money' did not follow the 'nigra'. It is important to understand the nature of his argument, because when we talk about a species being named in honour of someone, we mean that the person's name becomes part of the Latin name of the species. Thus *Phallus nikmoneyii* would be a plausible tribute to me from one of my students who discovered an unknown stinkhorn. Lloyd was not upset by this second practice. Quite a few fungi have the Latin name *lloydii*, and he would have appreciated my imaginary mushroom because he was an expert on stinkhorns, or 'phalloids', as he referred to them.

Curtis was the youngest of three brothers who established Lloyd Brothers Pharmacists in Cincinnati. The success of this venture made him wealthy and when he left the operation of the company to his brothers in 1905, he was free to pursue his interest in mycology. Curtis had been introduced to the study of fungi in the 1880s by a local naturalist, A. P. Morgan, who documented the 'mycologic flora' of the Miami Valley in Ohio. Free from the responsibilities of the pharmaceutical business, Curtis assembled and photographed a vast collection of herbarium specimens of fungi, described more than a thousand new species, and founded an extraordinary scientific library. Classical studies on fungi and plants purchased from European book dealers became the foundation of the Lloyd Library in Cincinnati, which remains a leading resource for botanical and pharmacological research.[4] In fact, a good deal of this book was written in the Lloyd Library.

Curtis Gates Lloyd, Cincinnati mycologist with an abiding interest in phallic mushrooms.

Curtis enjoyed an active social life as a young Cincinnatian. His correspondence, archived at the Lloyd Library, includes playful notes from women who accompanied him to dances and the opera. A few of these women appear to have hoped for a marriage proposal, but Curtis, like Buller, remained a bachelor. He had a well-developed sense of humour for his time, expressed in photographic portraits on greetings cards that showed him toasting the viewer with a foaming glass of beer; posing between two bare-breasted native women in Samoa (in an image faked in a photographic lab); and showing his weight gain between 1880 and 1906, 'before and after the study of fungi'.

His dismissive attitude towards the norms of gentlemanly behaviour is clear in the editorials he wrote for his own journal of mycology, *Mycological Notes*, which gave him a platform to attack professors who had little opportunity to defend themselves. He harried one poor botanist at Cornell, whom he indicted for describing a new genus based on a single specimen of a fruit body pickled in alcohol. Lloyd ridiculed this academic through the published correspondence of a fictitious mycologist, Professor McGinty, who entertained readers of *Mycological Notes* by making up ridiculous pretexts for naming mushrooms. The Cornell botanist was guilty as charged, but Curtis was sadistic in the pleasure he took in humiliating him with McGinty. On a more positive note, Lloyd used his journal to celebrate the careers of mycologists. Buller visited Curtis in Cincinnati in 1924, and became the subject of one of Curtis's brief biographies. Their correspondence suggests that they enjoyed a friendship born from mutual professional respect, which was made easier because Buller had no interest in naming anything.

Advances in mycology in the twentieth century allowed the study of fungal biology to follow specialized lines of investigation and there have been few scientists who have contributed to multiple subject areas like Buller did. Authors of comprehensive mycology textbooks, including Constantine Alexopoulos, John

Elsie Wakefield, Head of Mycology at Kew for 40 years, and C. T. Ingold, influential mycologist who studied mechanisms of spore release for more than 70 years.

Burnett and John Webster, probably had the greatest impact on the study of fungi after Buller.

John Corner (1906–1996) was a British mycologist whose diplomatic skills helped to protect the Singapore Botanic Gardens during the Japanese occupation of the island in the Second World War. As a student at Cambridge, Corner had considered suicide in response to a personal assessment of his ignorance of science. Driven to overcome these shortcomings, he went on to become an exacting botanist and influential mycologist who made significant discoveries about spore development and the anatomy of bracket fungi. In his study of the tropical flora in Singapore, Corner developed methods for training macaques to collect plant specimens from the tree canopy. The hazards of this enterprise became evident when he was attacked and severely injured by one of his 'botanical monkeys'. The resulting disability prevented him from entering military service against the Japanese and in his memoirs he credited the vicious macaque with saving his life.

C. T. Ingold (1905–2010) was another extraordinary mycologist, whose studies on spore discharge spanned seventy years.[5]

His popular books on fungi influenced generations of students. Other scientists made spectacular discoveries about fungi, or, rather, used fungi to make spectacular discoveries in medicine, molecular genetics and cell biology. Some of them won Nobel Prizes. It is too soon to consider the long-term impact of the mushroom experts of my generation, but the scientists who developed the molecular phylogenetic approaches that have clarified our picture of fungal evolution are of definite prominence.

This selection of academic mycologists may seem snobbish to readers who have learned a great deal from enthusiasts who do not hold doctorates in fungal biology. By sharing their enormous wisdom, authors of books on mushroom identification and cookery have played very important roles in educating people about fungi. Other mushroom aficionados stray too far into wishful thinking about the power of fungi to treat illnesses and solve environmental problems. Devotees of magic mushrooms occupy another cultural niche.

Relatively little attention has been given to women scientists who have shaped the study of mycology.[6] Too much has been made of the early investigations on fungi by children's author Beatrix Potter. She was one of the millions of women faced with limited professional opportunities in the late nineteenth century, and we have allowed her celebrity to boost her posthumous reputation as an amateur scientist.[7] The emancipation of women after the First World War made things better in Europe, and Elsie Wakefield was an early beneficiary. The effect of the continuing gender bias in the sciences is not a sufficient explanation for the indifference towards women's contributions to the field in the twentieth century. The reason few female mycologists are celebrated in snippets of biography is because their professional mishaps provide scant entertainment. It seems unlikely that an unmarried woman who lived in a hotel, wrote poems about fungi and strapped horse blinders to her head would have enjoyed a successful career in the 1920s.

*eight*

# Mushroom Ecology

When we consider the ecology of mushrooms, it is the colony or mycelium, rather than the fruit body, that is the subject of inquiry. The fruit body is a source of food for some animals and serves as a nursery for developing insect larvae, but it does not affect the development of the surrounding plants. Mushrooms shed spores. They do not do anything else. It is the mycelia from which mushrooms develop that are the critical players in ecology, making immense contributions to the global cycling of chemical elements. Mycelia of many mushroom species connect with plant roots and engage in associations called mycorrhizas that support the fungus and the plant. Mushrooms whose mycelia decompose fallen timber and other dead plant tissues are called saprotrophs. Mycorrhizal mushrooms and saprotrophs are the subject of this chapter. Other mushroom species feed by attacking living plants. The activities of these parasitic fungi are the main subject of the next chapter.

Mycorrhizas are symbiotic partnerships between fungi and plants.[1] The term 'symbiosis' refers to any manner of close physical relationship between two or more species. Mycorrhizas are examples of mutualistic symbioses, from which both players benefit. Parasitism is a contrasting form of symbiosis that favours one organism at the expense of the other. In a third kind of symbiosis, called commensalism, one organism benefits from interacting with another species without causing it any obvious harm. It can be difficult to judge whether an interaction is mutualistic or parasitic when the costs and benefits of the relationship are not obvious. The situation is complicated further in organisms that switch from mutualism to parasitism. The edible matsutake

Mycorrhizal root tips of a coniferous tree colonized by a species of *Amanita*.

mushroom, *Tricholoma matsutake*, is an example of a fungus that turns on its plant partners. It begins by establishing supportive mycorrhizas with young roots, then switches to attacking its host, and completes the interaction by decomposing the tissues of the dead plant.

Mycorrhizal mushrooms associated with broadleaf trees, conifers and woody shrubs form a particular kind of symbiosis called an ectomycorrhiza. Mycelia of a lot of the most familiar mushrooms form these associations. Species of *Amanita*, *Cortinarius* (webcaps), *Lactarius* (milkcaps), *Russula* and *Boletus* are all dependent upon their ectomycorrhizal relationships with trees. The connection between fungi and plants can be seen by brushing the soil away from the tips of tree roots in a conifer plantation. Roots colonized by fungi have short, stubby branches. An exterior sleeve or mantle of fungal hyphae covering these branches will be apparent when the root tips are inspected with a hand lens. In the undisturbed root, this mantle is attached to the mycelium,

An example of a mycorrhizal cheater, the orchid *Hexalectris spicata*, which obtains food from fungi in its roots that connect with other plants through conventional mycorrhizal associations.

which spreads through the soil. Under the mantle, the mycelium spreads between the cells in the outer layer of root tissue, creating a web of filaments called the Hartig net. The external mycelium absorbs water and dissolved minerals from the soil and feeds the plant through this Hartig net. The benefit to the mushroom comes from sugars produced by the plant that flow in the opposite direction through the Hartig net.

*Amanita* species form ectomycorrhizas with many different plant species. Other mushrooms, including species of *Leccinum* and *Suillus*, which are boletes, are more finicky, and associate with a single plant species. Multiple plants in a forest can be connected through the same mycelium, establishing a common mycorrhizal network. This enables nutrients to be shared between plants in the network. Some networks are exploited by parasitic plants that lack chlorophyll. The roots of these 'mycorrhizal cheaters' derive food from fungi that colonize their roots without contributing any sugars themselves. Orchids that lack chlorophyll are examples of these freeloaders. Most species of orchid are green and they form a unique type of mycorrhizal association with mushroom mycelia, in which the hyphae of the fungus grow as coils inside the cells of the orchid root. These coils are digested by the orchid to obtain food. The fungus obtains its food by participating in a mycorrhizal network or from the decomposition of wood. Germination of the tiny seeds of orchids is dependent on association with a fungus, because the seeds do not have enough stored food to support the early development of the plant. As the plant grows and begins to make its own food by photosynthesis, the reliance on the fungus decreases and the plant begins to feed the fungus with sugars.

Mycorrhizal mushrooms are vital for sustaining healthy forests. Pines, spruces and larches, which dominate the northern boreal forests of Canada and Russia, are supported by ectomycorrhizal symbioses. Ectomycorrhizas also support trees in temperate and tropical forests. The mycelia of these fungi can spread through a large volume of soil, operating as accessory root systems for their plant partners. Hyphae release acids as they extend through the soil, which leach calcium, magnesium and other elements from rocks. These elements tend to be very scarce in the soil and are crucial for plant growth. The hyphae can also access nitrogen by decomposing the scraps of protein in dead insects. Studies have shown that the mycorrhizal mushroom *Laccaria bicolor* supplies pine trees with nitrogen obtained by killing soil invertebrates called springtails.[2]

When the genome of *Laccaria bicolor* was sequenced, investigators found that the fungus lacked the enzymes that decompose the cell walls of plants.[3] This was an interesting finding, because other evidence shows that mycorrhizal mushrooms evolved from saprotrophic species. During the evolution of mycorrhizal relationships, these mushrooms must have lost the machinery for decomposing the cell wall materials that constitute wood. These fungi have not become entirely dependent on their host plants and can supplement their diet by breaking down non-woody organic matter in the soil.

Saprotrophs that do not make any connections with plant roots include the horsehair mushroom, *Marasmius rotula*, whose fruit bodies sprout from thin twigs buried in leaf litter. The name 'horsehair mushroom' refers to the tough, black stem of the fruit body. The caps of this species are pure white, no more than 2 cm in diameter and often much smaller, with wide-spaced gills. Inspection with a hand lens reveals the beautiful symmetrical arrangement of the gills, which look like spokes on a tiny wheel that connect to a hub encircling the top of the stem. Clusters of larger fruit bodies that grow from fallen logs include the bleeding mycena, *Mycena haematopus*, whose flesh exudes drops of 'blood' when it is damaged. Other evocative names for this fungus are the bleeding fairy helmet and the burgundydrop bonnet. The fruit bodies of this mushroom become covered sometimes with the glassy hairs of a parasitic fungus called *Spinellus fusiger*, a

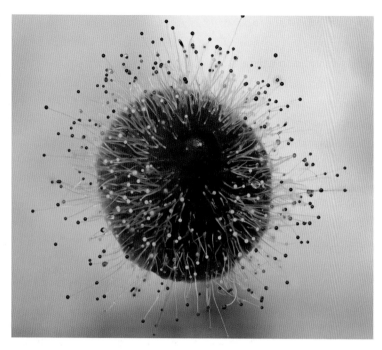

Filaments tipped with spores produced by the parastitic fungus *Spinellus fusiger* on the cap of a *Mycena* fruit body.

kind of pin mould. This illustrates the way in which the tissues of mushrooms involved in wood decay are themselves subject to putrefaction. Everything decomposes.

Brown rot fungi break down the cellulose in wood and leave the dark lignin behind. White rot fungi decompose cellulose and lignin. Lignin forms a tough scaffold around the cellulose fibres and is not consumed by mycelia for energy. The mechanism of wood decomposition used by white rot mushrooms requires them to clear away the lignin to expose the cellulose for digestion. Mycelia of brown rot mushrooms have evolved a workaround that enables them to get at the cellulose without removing the lignin. This strategy may save energy. The categories of brown and white rot oversimplify the diverse physiological mechanisms used in wood decomposition, but they are a good starting point in thinking about how saprotrophic mycelia work.

Many of the mushrooms that decompose wood do not produce fruit bodies with a classic umbrella shape. Widespread species of shelf or bracket fungi include the sulphur shelf, *Laetiporus sulphureus*, whose bright golden-yellow projections are easily spotted in the woods, and a pair of less conspicuous mushrooms called the turkey tail, *Trametes versicolor*, and false turkey tail, *Stereum ostrea*. The turkey tail and false turkey tail produce large numbers of thin shelves that jut from the sides of rotting logs. Both have patterns of concentric rings on their upper surfaces like the tail fans of wild turkeys. Sulphur shelves and turkey tails have pores on the underside of their fruit bodies, whereas the pale bottom of the false turkey tail is smooth. Sulphur shelf is an edible brown rot fungus; both turkey tails are white rotters.

The beefsteak fungus, *Fistulina hepatica*, and the oyster mushroom, *Pleurotus ostreatus*, can also be described as shelf fungi, but they sometimes support their curved caps with rudimentary stems. The beefsteak fungus releases its spores from rubbery tubes that are separated from one another rather than fused into a surface of pores. Oyster mushrooms have white gills. Both species are edible and the oyster is cultivated on sawdust and agricultural waste, including rice straw. Other saprotrophic mushrooms include crust fungi, whose flattened fruit bodies fuse

Beefsteak fungus, *Fistulina hepatica*.

Rhizomorphs or 'bootlaces' of *Armillaria mellea* exposed by removal of bark from a dead Norway spruce.

with the surface of fallen logs. The term 'resupinate' is also used to describe crust fungi. *Irpex lacteus*, which does not have a colloquial name, is a widespread species whose scruffy white crusts support irregular flattened teeth or are pockmarked with pores. *Phanerochaete chrysosporium* is another common crust fungus that produces a yellowish fruit body. These fungi tend to grow on the bottom of logs or wrap themselves upwards onto the sides of the decaying wood, and drop their spores from pores or teeth. A metre-long crust on the underside of an oak log discovered in 2010 in old-growth tropical woodland on Hainan Island in China is the largest recorded fruit body.[4] It is produced by a white rot fungus called *Phellinus ellipsoideus*, weighs 500 kg and releases a trillion spores per day from hundreds of millions of tubes.

*Phanerochaete* and other wood-decay mushrooms produce bundles of filamentous hyphae called mycelial cords and rhizomorphs that can transport water and dissolved nutrients over many metres of soil. These root-like structures allow the fungi to redistribute water and nutrients across the mycelium from a source of active decay to places where the mycelium is searching for fresh wood. Species of *Armillaria*, or honey fungus, produce black rhizomorphs that are called bootlaces. Masses of these can be found under the bark of rotting trees.

Looking up into the crowns of dead and dying trees, we find shelf fungi, which include the enormous fruit bodies of the artist's fungus, *Ganoderma applanatum*, which also grows on logs after they fall to the ground, the hoof fungus, *Fomes fomentarius*, and dryad's saddle, *Polyporus squamosus*. The mycelia of these white rot mushrooms often begin growing as parasites on living trees and continue to destroy the wood after the host plants have died.

Grasses and other non-woody plant tissues are an alternative source of food for saprotrophic mushrooms. A number of species with small fruit bodies thrive on the partly decomposed plant tissues in compost, rotting hay and manure. Fruit bodies of ink caps and the related mottlegills, which are species of *Panaeolus*, are common on herbivore dung. Other mushrooms that populate pastures benefit from the soil enrichment provided by cows, sheep and horses, even though they do not fruit directly from their dung.

Fruit body of the dry rot fungus, *Serpula lacrymans*.

Brown rot mushrooms cause wood decay in homes. In Europe, dry rot is caused by *Serpula lacrymans*, which forms conspicuous black cords as it explores the spaces between kitchen tiles and creeps along wood joists. This fungus follows the brown rot programme of wood decomposition and causes hardwood beams to crumble into brown cubes. *Meruliporia incrassata* causes the same kind of home damage in the western United States, where its destructive rhizomorphs can grow as thick as garden hosepipes. *Serpula* and *Meruliporia* fruit bodies develop as crusts on the surface of the decomposing wood.

Dry rot had a devastating effect on the old oak-hulled battleships of the Royal Navy, even destroying vessels in dock before they were launched. Part of the problem lay in the dwindling supply of timber in Britain after the Reformation and the importation of unseasoned wood from Eastern Europe. Damage to the battleships continued for centuries and peaked during the Napoleonic Wars (1799–1815), before the losses were controlled, to some degree, by the development of creosote as a wood preservative. *Neolentinus lepideus* is a mushroom with a scaly cap that grows on conifer stumps and on fence posts treated with creosote and other wood preservatives. It has earned the name train wrecker from its development on railway sleepers (ties in America), though there is no evidence that it has caused any accidents.

The decomposition of human artefacts by fungi highlights the fact of our inescapable participation in the carbon cycle. Everything that we manufacture from natural products, as well as many plastics and other synthetic materials, will be broken down, eventually, into carbon dioxide and water by fungi and other microorganisms. The chair on which you are sitting will disappear one day, as well as the roof over your head, everyone you will ever know, and all that you will ever be. This does not have to be a source of gloom. A foray in the woods after rainfall to look at the fungi that live by decomposition can, with a little reflection, become a life-affirming experience. *Carpe diem.*

# nine

# Mushroom Parasites

Mushrooms loom large in popular culture as agents of decomposition, but are not as well known as the cause of disease and death. This is not surprising, because most of them are saprotrophs, whose colonies rot leaf litter and dissolve the trunks of fallen trees. The minority of mushrooms that attack perfectly healthy plants have 'learned' how to overcome the defensive mechanisms that operate in living tissues and are then able to feed on their debilitated hosts. Mushrooms that infect other mushrooms and species that kill nematode worms have also undergone evolutionary modifications that allow them to damage their prey. Rare infections of human tissues by mushroom colonies are the unfortunate consequences of chance encounters in which the fungus escapes destruction by the immune system. These infections do not result from any evolutionary fine-tuning of mycelial behaviour that helps mushrooms to harm us. In this chapter we will consider mushrooms that attack plants, other mushrooms, soil invertebrates and humans.

A little reddish mushroom threatens the world's supply of cocoa pods, whose seeds are refined into the raw ingredient of chocolate.[1] (Cacao is the preferred spelling, and comes from a Spanish noun, but cocoa is less jarring to English speakers and is used widely.) This fungus, *Moniliophthora perniciosa*, causes the disease witches' broom in cocoa and nightmares for cocoa farmers. The gills of this tropical fungus are spaced widely, like spokes on a bicycle wheel. It is a member of the same family as the horsehair mushroom, *Marasmius rotula*, which grows from small dead twigs. Spores shed from this pretty fruit body germinate on cocoa trees and establish invasive filaments in the leafy branches, flowers and the

Fruit body of *Moniliophthora perniciosa*, the pathogenic fungus that causes witches' broom of cocoa.

pods. The mycelium disrupts the hormonal balance within the plant, causing it to form stunted branches with crowded leaves. 'Broom' refers to the resemblance between the brushy ends of infected branches and the aircraft piloted by witches.

The fungus attacks wild cocoa trees in its rainforest home in South America, where the number of infections are limited by the low density of vulnerable plants. When an infection takes hold in a single cultivar of cocoa grown in crowded plantations of trees of precisely the same age, the crop does not stand a chance. The earliest report of the disease came from a Brazilian explorer in the 1780s, who found the misshapen growths on cocoa cultivated deep in the Amazon basin. A century later, Dutch plantations in Surinam were devastated by the fungus, and witches' broom spread to other cocoa-producing countries in South America. Ecuadorian 'cocoa kings' who had enjoyed farcical wealth, illustrated by their purported preference for sending their shirts to be laundered in Paris, were bankrupted by the arrival of the fungus early in the twentieth century. Plantations in eastern Brazil escaped the disease until the 1980s, but crops have been devastated in recent years. West Africa is the centre of chocolate production today and, so far, the fungus has stayed on the other side of the Atlantic Ocean.

The impact of disease outbreaks can be managed by careful pruning of deformed branches, but there is a limit to how many of the infected brooms can be removed before a butchered tree becomes useless. The fungus tolerates dense sprayings of fungicides and the greatest hope for disease control lies in breeding resistant cultivars of cocoa. The options are depressing for small farming operations challenged by the slimmest margin between profit and devastation. There is little ground for optimism in this story, but with the global market for cocoa approaching $100 billion, the conflict between growers and fungus is inescapable.

Other mushrooms that cause plant disease include species of *Armillaria*, or honey fungus, which attack tree roots. Honey fungi have very catholic tastes in plants, infecting the root systems of hundreds of species of shrubs and trees. Once they have invaded a plant, they can spread to its neighbours through the soil or via natural grafts that connect entire stands of trees. The fungus specializes in destroying roots and does not grow into the stem or branches at all. Nevertheless, the breakdown of root systems leads to the swift dispatch of shrubs and trees. A honey fungus mycelium begins life by infecting a single plant and then spreads outwards along all compass points, searching for susceptible plants. In addition to migrating through root grafts, the fungus uses its cords or rhizomorphs to travel through soil until it hits another root. This explains how honey mushroom mycelia can grow for thousands of years, producing expansive colonies that are considered among the largest and oldest organisms in the world. Fruiting takes place periodically at different locations within the colony, producing the characteristic yellow-tinged mushrooms responsible for the common name. Young fruit bodies of *Armillaria* are popular edible mushrooms in parts of Europe, and in Ukraine and Russia. Some experts warn against eating this mushroom because it can cause a stomach upset.

*Heterobasidion annosum*, which attacks conifers, works in a similar way to the honey fungus. An outbreak of 'annosum root rot' in a forestry plantation gets started when spores of this fungus germinate on a freshly cut tree stump. The mycelium spreads to the root system of the cut tree and travels to connecting trees through root grafts. Once it finds itself in an uncut tree, the fungus grows upwards into the base or 'butt' of the trunk, rotting a good deal of the heartwood before any disease symptoms are visible on the outside. It cannot travel far through soil because it does not produce cords, but it is a terrifically damaging fungus. *Heterobasidion* ranks as the most important forest pathogen in the northern hemisphere.

Many of the fungi that rot the heartwood of standing trees begin their interactions with plants by feeding on living tissues before they switch to saprotrophic growth on dead wood. These fungi often invade wounds on older trees. Wood-rotting mushrooms slide between the categories of parasite and saprotroph, just as some of the mycorrhizal fungi transition to attacking their partners and then feeding on their dead remains. Further complexity is introduced by the way that some biologists use the terms 'pathogen' and 'parasite'. The distinction is tricky. Parasite is the preferred term for a fungus, like the cause of witches' broom, which feeds on the living tissues of its hosts and then becomes aggressive and kills the plant. Pathogen is an alternative that does not come with the connotation of a protracted relationship before the act of murder.

Mushrooms that attack trees through wounds and dead branches include *Phellinus igniarius*, which infects birch and alder. *Phellinus* grows up and down the trunk, decomposing the heartwood for ten or twenty years before releasing spores from hardened conks, shaped like hooves, on the trunk of the dying tree. There is a tradition among Native Americans in western Alaska of mixing the ashes of burnt conks with tobacco, and chewing this concoction for an elevated nicotine 'kick'.

The sulphur shelf, *Laetiporus sulphureus*, is a mushroom with pores that infects living trees and continues to grow after the host has died. *Climacodon septentrionalis* is often found in the same woods as the sulphur shelf. It forms pure white brackets on broadleaved trees but is easy to miss because they can grow high up on the trunk towards the crown. An unusual feature of this mushroom is the formation of long spines that point downwards below the cap. The infectious basidiospores develop on the surface of the spines and are spread by the wind.

Plants are not the only prey for pathogenic fungi. Fungi that attack other fungi are called mycoparasites and a few of them are mushrooms. Mycoparastic mushrooms feed on fruit body tissues and produce their own fruit bodies on these damaged platforms. Acts of fungus eating fungus have been described as cannibalism, but this is a gross misreading of nature. Some parasitic mushrooms and their mushroom victims are related more distantly than are vampire bats to the Archbishop of Canterbury. Species of *Asterophora* attack *Russula nigricans* and other mushrooms late in the development of their hosts, producing clusters of white fruit bodies. *Asterophora* and *Russula*, like bats and archbishops, are classified in different taxonomic orders. Species of

Parasitic mushroom *Asterophora lycoperdoides* fruiting on the rotten cap of *Russula nigricans*.

the parasitic jelly fungus *Tremella* reach even deeper into the tree of life, attacking a broad range of mushrooms from which they are separated by an expanse of evolutionary history. Because *Tremella* species, including yellow witches' butter, *Tremella mesenterica*, grow on rotting wood, they look like wood-decay fungi, but they feed by tapping into the mycelia and fruit bodies of other mushrooms that are actually decomposing the wood.

Species of *Hebeloma* include the poison pie, *Hebeloma crustuliniforme*, and the much rarer Australian ghoul fungus, *Hebeloma aminophilum*, which grows on animal carcasses. Hebelomas (there is no common name) are abused by species of another mushroom called *Squamanita,* which transform their hosts into monstrous lumps of unrecognizable tissue. The attack is so vicious that its victims can be identified only from their genetic remains.[2] *Squamanita* extends its services to other mushrooms including the powder cap, *Cystoderma amianthinum,* where it is known as the powder cap strangler. In this case, the parasite uses the infected stem of the powder cap as the base of the stalk for its own mushroom. *Squamanita* and *Cystoderma* are close relatives. Another parasitic interaction between close relatives includes the growth of poroid mushrooms of *Pseudoboletus parasiticus* on the earth-ball *Scleroderma citrinum.* Although earth-balls look like puffballs, genetic analysis places them in the same order as the boletes.

Mycelia of some common mushrooms that decompose organic matter in soil also invest energy in slaying nematodes and other invertebrates. The payback for the mushroom is unclear. It is possible that this activity provides the fungus with a source of nitrogen, but it could also serve as a defensive mechanism against pests that feed on the mycelium. The large ink cap called lawyer's wig or shaggy mane, *Coprinus comatus,* is one of the fungi skilled in

*Pseudoboletus parasiticus* (on left) fruiting from common earth-balls, *Scleroderma citrinum.*

*Schizophyllum commune*, fruiting on wood. This mushroom is known as 'split gill', referring to the divided structure of the gills. The two halves of each gill curl apart as they dry and unroll to meet a single blade when they rehydrate. This may be an adaptation that allows the fungus to resume spore release after periods of dry weather. In rare cases, this species causes infections of human nasal sinuses.

killing nematode worms.[3] It deploys a dual strategy against the worms, in which the mycelium produces tiny spiked balls on its surface and secretes toxins. The spikes rip the skin of the worms as they glide by, exposing their wounded tissues to the toxins. Toxins are also marshalled against worms by the oyster mushroom, *Pleurotus ostreatus*, and a common lawn mushroom, *Conocybe lactea*. Pest control is a fascinating addition to the repertoire of ecological functions performed by mushroom mycelia. The phenomenon has not been examined in many species and is probably more widespread than we recognize.

Infections of humans by mushroom mycelia are very rare, but when they do occur they can be difficult to treat.[4] Plenty of mushroom spores find themselves in our nasal passages and lungs. This is inevitable given the global distribution of millions of tons of these particles in the atmosphere. Some of the spores probably germinate in the lung, but they are destroyed by the protective macrophages of the immune system that police our tissues, and are expelled in the continuous flow of mucilage from the lung.

The split gill mushroom, *Schizophyllum commune*, is one of the culprits in these extraordinary 'mycoses' and has been found in infections of the nasal sinuses. This is a wood-rotting basidio-mycete with no obvious adaptations for growth in animal tissues. A few of these infections have been reported in patients with healthy immune systems, which makes it difficult to understand how the infection began in the first place. Most fungal infections occur when the immune system is impaired by viral infection or cancer therapy. The exposure of our innards during surgery is another invitation to fungi, and mycelial growth on replace-ment heart valves is one of the horrors reported in the medical literature. Ink caps are among the fungi that show up in these extraordinary case histories.

Infections caused by fungi that produce mushrooms represent a tiny fraction of the catalogue of human mycoses. Plenty of other types of fungi are more common causes of human disease. We are food for a profusion of these microorganisms when our immune systems fail. Indeed, a recent study of medical statistics estimated that more than 170 people die every hour from fungal infections.[5] Enough of this horror. Human prey becomes predator in the next chapter, as we turn to the joys of mushroom picking.

Copperplate engraving from Sterbeeck's *Theatrum fungorum* showing a variety of mushrooms in a pastoral scene.

## *ten*
# Mushroom Picking

Wild mushrooms supplement the diets of people in many countries and intensive picking has become a commercial enterprise in regions where the most desirable species are found. Natural history enthusiasts in Europe and North America have adopted mushrooming as a hobby and enjoy cooking their quarry after a foray in the woods. Bird watching is a comparable pastime, although it is more popular than mushrooming and few bird experts, I expect, long secretly to eat the birds that they glimpse through their binoculars or wish to collect their eggs. In this respect, mushroomers bear greater similarity to animal hunters, with the difference that bloodlust is limited among people who fill their baskets with fragrant fruit bodies. We will explore the different expressions of mushrooming in this chapter, from the enjoyment of weekend hobbyists who meet for mushroom forays to the business of large-scale commercial picking.

The need to provide an authoritative guide for mushroom picking was an important impetus for Renaissance studies of mushrooms. *Theatrum fungorum*, published by Franciscus van Sterbeeck in 1675, was the first book devoted wholly to mushrooms. Sterbeeck was a Flemish priest and member of the nobility who spent most of his life in Antwerp. A century later, an Italian priest, Giovanni Battarra, published a splendid set of engravings of mushrooms in his study of fungi that grew around Rimini. Mycological studies with hand-coloured plates began to appear towards the end of the eighteenth century and were helpful in distinguishing between mushrooms that in uncoloured engravings looked almost identical.

Most modern mushroom guidebooks illustrate fungi with colour photographs, but there are some very good sources that continue to employ watercolour paintings of fruit bodies. Drawings and paintings can be more useful than photographs for identifying some species because a single illustration can incorporate the peculiarities of many individual specimens. A single photograph cannot offer this kind of synthetic view of a mushroom. Some of the same reasoning applies to the choice of paintings over photographs by authors of standard ornithological guides. Websites concerned with mushroom identification can circumvent this limitation of photography by showing multiple specimens from different angles to help in identification.[1]

A good guidebook is essential for mushroom pickers, and time spent with an expert teacher is the best way to learn the science

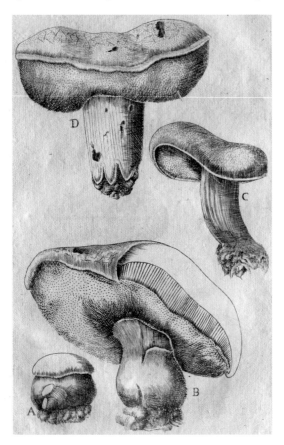

Boletus in an uncoloured engraving from the 18th century.

and art of mushroom recognition. A magnifying glass or hand lens is another indispensable tool, needed to examine details of fruit body structure, and a pocketknife with a curved blade is useful for unearthing mushrooms or cutting them from logs. Mushroom identification can be very difficult. Part of the challenge is created by the variability between the shapes and sizes of fruit bodies of the same species, which brings us back to the shortcomings of photographic portraits.

Excellent foraging can happen in unassuming locations. Twenty years ago, following a tip from a local botanist, I visited a river gorge or 'hollow' cut through rock in western Kentucky. This was a spot favoured by locals for fishing and it was littered with

*Boletus* in a hand-coloured plate from the 18th century.

discarded bottles and other refuse and had been used as an illegal dump for old kitchen appliances and television sets. Along the riverbanks, however, deep in the gorge, the vegetation rioted and mushrooms were fruiting everywhere. The rock walls of the hollow trapped warm air, creating a tropical microclimate that aroused a madness of fungi. ('Madness' is proposed as a collective noun for a mass fruiting of wild mushrooms.) With every step I found more mushrooms. I found myself thinking of common species that I had not seen that day, and then finding them a few minutes later. This was a bewitching place, a mycological paradise, ravaged by the people who treated it as a rubbish tip. On the flip side of this inspirational foray are the many disappointing trips that I have taken to places renowned for the richness of their fungi. The explanation for these failed pursuits is that fruiting is subject to weather conditions and a dry spell can halt all the new flushes. Rainfall in the days before a foray is the most favourable omen for a productive hunt.

Tools of the trade: a mushroom knife with a curved blade, and a hand lens.

Unlike ornithologists, who are likely to see most of the birds in a particular location if they are patient, mushroomers miss the majority of fungi wherever they look. We find the species that are fruiting, but the mycelia of so many others are growing in the soil and leaf litter without forming fruit bodies. To begin to formulate a complete picture of the diversity of fungi we need to visit the same spot repeatedly. Even then, species that fruit very rarely are likely to be overlooked. Genetic research can help identify these cryptic fungi. This involves amplifying the genes from mycelia hidden in the soil and looking for matches with species whose DNA sequences are archived in a computer database. By recognizing our blindness to the true diversity of organisms we can feel liberated by the richness of the invisible biology. I have used the phrase *The Amoeba in the Room* for a book title that refers to the invisible majority of life.[2]

Fruit body size, shape and colour are the most obvious clues for identifying a mushroom. Odour is useful in a few cases. Mushroom smells can be similar to apricots, almonds, garlic, bleach or anise, and others are described as fishy, mealy or, simply, 'mushroomy' – like a white button mushroom. Older guidebooks refer to the taste of little pieces of fruit body, but taste tests cannot be recommended when there is a possibility of swallowing tissue from a toxic species. Details of mushroom structure are very useful in identification. These include the presence of a ring, or annulus, around the stem; scales or warts on top of the cap; and a cup, or volva, at the base of the stem. A web, or cortina, stretched under the cap indicates that the mushroom may be a species of *Cortinarius*, and drops of milky sap exuded from a damaged fruit body are characteristic of *Lactarius*. Slimy caps are also helpful for identification. The shape and arrangement of gills is another important character and this requires familiarity with technical terms like 'adnate' and 'adnexed' when comparing descriptions of species in a guidebook. Spore colours are useful, but unless the mushroom has left a deposit of spores beneath its cap a spore print is needed, and this cannot be made in the woods.

There is an art to knowing which features of the specimen are useful and which can be ignored. Even an expert can be stumped by fungi in the field and have to look at details of spore shape and size using a microscope. Chemical tests are also used to resolve difficult species. These include colour changes caused by adding a drop of ammonia, potassium hydroxide or iodine to a mushroom cap. The good news for lovers of mushroom cooking is that it is relatively easy to spot the deadly poisonous species. Death caps and destroying angels have the rings on their stems and cups at the base of their fruit bodies. Many non-toxic *Amanita* species have these characteristics, including a few edible mushrooms, but it makes sense to avoid all amanitas unless you are an *Amanita* specialist. The same goes for webcaps: some of the species of *Cortinarius* are poisonous, so it is best to keep all of them out of the kitchen. Never eat any mushroom when there is any question about its identity.

Weekend mushroom forays can attract hundreds of participants interested in learning about fungi, meeting people with similar interests, getting outdoors and enjoying a wild mushroom feast. The sustainability of mushroom picking is an emotive issue for field mycologists. People who gather mushrooms from nature for personal consumption are unlikely to do significant damage to a fungal population. Commercial picking is a different matter. Seasonal mushroom markets are common in France and other European countries and the love of wild mushrooms in many cultures pre-dates the Roman Empire. As long as the majority of the mushroom harvest is consumed within the country of origin, over-picking is limited. With the exception of French truffles, trade in most wild mushrooms has been limited to local markets until quite recently. Global commerce changes everything and the impact of international trade on natural populations of fungi is difficult to determine. The Pacific Northwest of the United States

Different types
of gill attachment
used for identi-
fying mushroom
species: A, free;
B, decurrent; C,
adnate; D, notched;
E, adnexed.

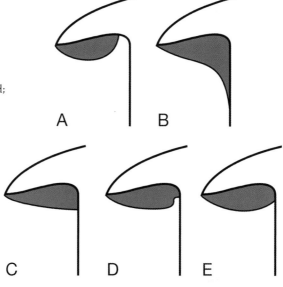

is one of the regions where mushroom picking takes place on a scale that may be unsustainable. Research on this harvest from the 1990s suggested that up to 2,000 tons of mushrooms were being picked every year with a value of tens of millions of dollars.[3] Intensive picking continues today. The haul is dominated by chanterelles and boletes, but the American matsutake or pine mushroom, *Tricholoma magnivalere*, is the most valuable fungus from this area and is exported to Japan. Matsutake is an ingredient in sukiyaki and is also fried to make a mushroom tempura. China has become the largest exporter of wild mushrooms, with a national harvest of hundreds of thousands of tons of fruit bodies annually.[4]

When a mushroom is picked, the underground mycelium is not affected directly. This fact has encouraged many mycologists to assume that picking does no damage to fungal populations and should not be regulated. There are some problems with this argument. Because mushrooms release spores, the act of removing the fruit body ensures that billions of spores will be lost. When a few fruit bodies are removed from a larger patch of mushrooms, the impact on spore numbers is going to be limited. But mushroom

Variety of coral mushrooms on display at a fungal foray.

colonies do not produce fruit bodies in order to donate a surplus of energy to the rest of nature. Each mushroom is a wager against the infinitesimal probability that a single spore will find a suitable place to initiate a new colony. If every mushroom from a colony is picked, the small chance of success becomes zero. Intensive picking is a damaging activity, just as overfishing is ruinous for a species of fish. The loss of genetic diversity is one of a number of potential challenges created by removing new generations of spores from the environment.[5]

Deleterious effects of picking have not been observed in the handful of published experiments on this topic. In one study in Switzerland that ran for almost thirty years, researchers found no evidence of changes in fruiting patterns from year to year when all of the edible mushrooms were removed from experimental plots.[6] Some caveats deserve consideration. Spores dispersed from fruit bodies outside the plots may have 'seeded' the picked areas, providing an injection of genetic variation that supported the health of mycelia. The duration of these experiments is another issue. Thirty years is a good chunk of a human lifespan, but means very little to a mycelium that can live for centuries. In the Swiss study, the scientists picked from some plots from a raised walkway. They found that when they walked on the plots, trampling of the soil reduced the number of mushrooms that fruited the following year. This short-term effect of soil compression, in itself, is reason for caution in unregulated picking. The author's viewpoint is not held widely, but the authoritative test is under way as you read this: with the immense numbers of wild mushrooms being picked in China, the perfect experiment is in progress. As long as the exports of wild mushrooms continue at the present pace, one can claim that commercial harvesting is sustainable.

Few mushroom enthusiasts are responsible for overharvesting fruit bodies, but there is a question about aesthetics when we think about an organized foray after which hundreds of mushrooms are displayed on tables. Any educational benefit from displaying fungi in this fashion is trumped by the act of looking carefully at living mushrooms where they are growing. And when the table of fruit bodies is swept into a rubbish bin after the foray, this seems very distasteful. It is an act of disrespect towards these beautiful organisms, and an unconscious expression, perhaps, of the myth of our dominion over nature. I am aware, of course, of my heightened sensitivity on this issue. Commercial picking is an issue of much greater importance than weekend foraying, and deforestation, pollution and climate change surely have a greater impact on the survival of mushroom populations than any form of picking. The effect of this environmental turbulence on the future of mushrooms is the topic of the last chapter, but next, we turn to mushroom farming.

Shiitake mushrooms, *Lentinula edodes*, cultivated on a maple log.

*eleven*

# Mushroom Growing

The earliest description of mushroom cultivation was written in China in the thirteenth century. Mushroom farming was one of many agricultural advances during the Song dynasty (960–1279), when metal ploughs were redesigned for reclaiming 'wasteland', massive irrigation projects were completed and new crops were introduced. The method of cultivating shiitake mushrooms on logs was included in a county record from this period, but was probably introduced much earlier. Agriculture was changing in Europe at the same time, but the deliberate farming of mushrooms does not seem to have been introduced in the West for another five hundred years, when the French began growing meadow mushrooms on manure. Modern methods for raising shiitake and white button mushrooms are very similar to these original practices.

Shiitake, whose Latin name is *Lentinula edodes*, is a wood-rotting fungus classified in the same taxonomic family (the Marasmiaceae) as the mushroom that causes witches' broom disease of cocoa and the horsehair mushroom that grows on twigs. The common name refers to its growth on the shii tree, *Castanopsis cuspidata*, which is one of the sources of the wood used to grow the mushroom in Japan. Logs from oaks and other deciduous trees also work very well. Shiitake is a white rot fungus, so it breaks down the cellulose and lignin in the wood, transforming it into a squashy white pulp. Cultivation begins with the inoculation of stacks of fresh logs with plugs of pure mycelium or 'spawn'. These are tamped into holes drilled into the wood. After inoculation, the holes are sealed with wax to exclude other fungi that might compete with the shiitake mycelium. The fungus grows in the

Velvet shanks, *Flammulina velutipes*, cultivated in low light in bottles to produce enokitake.

wood for up to two years before the logs are soaked in tanks of cold water to initiate fruiting. After soaking, the wet logs are moved inside a building and fruiting begins within a week or two, continuing for ten days. The logs will produce mushrooms three times a year for up to five years.[1]

In the 1970s, China produced only 6 per cent of the world's cultivated mushrooms. By 2011, China controlled 80 per cent of the $20 billion mushroom market.[2] The shiitake crop in China, estimated at 5 million tons in 2011, was matched by the production of oyster mushrooms. Like shiitake, the oyster mushroom, *Pleurotus ostreatus*, is a wood-decay fungus grown on logs. Other wood-rotting mushrooms cultivated in China include species of the jelly fungus *Auricularia*, known as wood ears, and *Flammulina velutipes*. Logs have been replaced with bags of sawdust for growing some of these fungi. Agricultural waste is also used for growing mushrooms. In nature, *Flammulina velutipes* produces gilled mushrooms with orange-brown caps, whose stems are clothed in soft hairs at the base. This explains the common name of the mushroom, which is velvet shank. Cultivated velvet shanks do not look like this at all. They are pure white, with long skinny stems topped with tiny unopened caps. This form of the mushroom is called enokitake in Japan and is produced by growing the fungus in bottles or plastic cylinders in low light levels. The fruit bodies do not become pigmented under these conditions, and the elevated levels of carbon dioxide around the close-packed fruit bodies promote stem elongation.

The white button mushroom, *Agaricus bisporus*, is a more finicky species than shiitake, oyster mushrooms and other wood-decay fungi. It has been tamed by feeding with a mixture of straw, animal manure and gypsum, but requires very careful husbandry in climate-controlled buildings designed specially for mushroom growing.[3] It is related to the field or meadow mushroom, *Agaricus campestris*, which has been gathered as a wild mushroom in Europe for centuries. In the eighteenth century, British gardeners used primordia of the meadow mushroom gathered from soil to inoculate beds of straw and horse dung. This method was more reliable than waiting for the fungus to appear in the fields and meant that the seasonal crop was no longer at the mercy of a spell of dry weather. Manure was also used to grow mushrooms in 'mushroom caves' in France, and almost 2,000 km of mushroom beds were cultivated in abandoned mines below the suburbs of Paris before the First World War. Pennsylvania Quakers were the first mushroom growers in the United States. To provide stable environmental conditions for their crops, American growers adopted methods of indoor mushroom cultivation in dedicated 'mushroom houses'.

A method for growing spawn from spores was developed at the Pasteur Institute in Paris in the 1890s, which allowed growers to experiment with different mushroom strains and find the most productive and flavourful varieties. Competition came from investigators at the U.S. Department of Agriculture who used mycelium from spent mushroom beds to inoculate fresh beds of compost. This is similar, in a microbiological sense, to using a sourdough starter to raise fresh bread dough. It is unclear when growers replaced the meadow mushroom, *Agaricus campestris*, with the button mushroom, *Agaricus bisporus*, but the domesticated species changed the whole business of mushroom farming, creating a homogeneous product recognized all over the world. *Agaricus bisporus* is a rarity in the wild, but the first cultivated strains probably came from fruit bodies or mycelium collected in Western Europe.

*Agaricus bisporus* has an unusual life cycle in which a single mycelium raised from a single basidiospore can produce fruit bodies without mating. This is a clonal mechanism of reproduction that ensures that each generation of spores contains an identical set of genes. The advantage of this behaviour is that growers can be confident in the consistency of their crops, but clonal reproduction also carries the risk of vulnerability to disease. White button mushrooms can be compared with bananas: all of the commercial yellow bananas belong to a single cultivar that has been grown since the 1960s, and this plant is vulnerable to attack by a virulent strain of a fungus called *Fusarium oxysporum*. Fruit bodies of white button mushrooms are similarly limited in genetic diversity and are plagued by microscopic fungi that cause wet bubble, dry bubble, brown spot, cobweb, mat disease, green mould and plaster mould. The mushrooms are also spoiled by bacteria that blotch and pit the caps, and by viruses, nematode worms and insects. Cultivated white buttons are too delicate by half to survive in nature.

Before inoculation with the fungus, the straw-manure mix is arranged in heaps and colonized by bacteria that concentrate nutrients through their metabolic activities and raise the temperature of the organic matter. Gypsum and other ingredients are added during this composting phase. In the next step of this complex process, the decomposing mixture is brought indoors, spread on pallets, and pasteurized by steaming to kill nematodes and other pests. Steaming does not kill everything, which is important because the remaining microorganisms 'condition' the compost by removing ammonia. After steaming, the compost is stacked on metal shelves in growing rooms and inoculated with button mushroom spawn raised on cereal grains. Within two to three weeks,

Bed of white button mushrooms, *Agaricus bisporus.*

the mycelium will spread throughout the compost and exhaust the nutrients. 'Pinning', which refers to the formation of tiny white mushroom primordia, is stimulated by casing the bed with a layer of peat and limestone, lowering the temperature in the growing rooms and increasing airflow. This ventilation reduces the levels of carbon dioxide and volatile organic compounds released by the mushrooms. Fruit bodies appear in a few weeks and three flushes can be picked from a typical bed. Mushroom breeders have developed a few varieties of *Agaricus bisporus,* including strains that produce the darker crimini mushrooms. Older fruit bodies of a brown strain are sold as portabellos or portabellas.

Until recently, *Agaricus bisporus* was the biggest-selling mushroom, but production of shiitake and oyster mushrooms is now outstripping white buttons. All the cultivated mushrooms mentioned in this chapter have relatively simple saprotrophic lifestyles. They are decomposer basidiomycetes. Many wild mushrooms harvested in the woods are mycorrhizal species whose dietary needs cannot be satisfied with logs and manure. Chanterelles, boletes and matsutake must establish partnerships with living trees before they will fruit. The same is true of truffles, which can be raised in plantations called truffières. Truffles are ascomycetes, more closely related to morels than the gilled mushrooms of basidiomycetes. Edible morels are often associated with living trees as mycorrhizal

Paddy straw mushroom, *Volvariella volvacea*, with cup or volva enclosing the base of the stem.

fungi, but can also grow as saprotrophs around dead trees and are common after forest fires. Methods for cultivating morels have been patented, but they are too complicated for most growers.

The diversification of consumer tastes has driven innovations in growing mushrooms on agricultural waste. These methods provide the dual service of food production and recycling organic materials. The paddy straw mushroom, *Volvariella volvacea*, is grown on rice straw and woodchips in East Asia and Southeast Asia. It is a big white mushroom with a ring on the stem and cup or volva that cradles the base. The effectiveness of agricultural waste as a food for mushroom cultivation has encouraged investigators to explore the uses of fungi for decontaminating soils that have been polluted by industrial activities. This concept, called mycoremediation, relies on the ability of fungi to grow in a polluted environment, absorbing toxic metals and breaking down poisonous organic compounds. When fruiting occurs, the toxins accumulated in the mycelium are transferred into the fruit bodies. Cropping and disposal of mushrooms produced from polluted ground would then, in theory, leave the soil cleaner. Mycelia of some mushrooms are capable of detoxifying pollutants from the oil and gas industries, organic wood preservatives, pesticides and explosives. Experiments have been conducted using woodchips impregnated with these materials and the use of this technology for decontaminating larger areas of soil is under investigation. The oyster mushroom is one of the most promising fungi in these trials.

The oyster mushroom and other white rot fungi are also candidates for 'second generation' biofuel production, in which the mycelium is used to process fibrous plant materials rich in cellulose and lignin. Current biofuel production relies on yeast to ferment sugars from sugar cane in Brazil and from corn (maize) in the u.s. This process would be revolutionized if mushroom mycelia could be used to release sugars from fibrous crop residues because this would open up a limitless supply of raw materials for ethanol production. Trials have been conducted in which oyster mushrooms are fed rice straw. Another experimental use of mushroom mycelia involves their addition to soil spoiled by mining activity. The hope for this biotechnological application is that the fungi will support plant health by enhancing soil fertility and establishing mycorrhizas. Mushroom mycelia have also been considered as agents for water purification, functioning as natural filters for removing pollutants and bacteria. Another creative application of mushroom mycelia has been their use to grow bricks for building construction. Mycelium of the lingzhi or reishi mushroom, *Ganoderma lucidum*, cultivated on crop residues in brick-shaped moulds produces dense white blocks. After oven-drying, the lightweight blocks offer remarkable compressive strength. Mycelial bricks are fire-resistant and, unlike bricks made from clay, they are biodegradable. This emerging technology can seem fanciful, but cow dung and other natural products have been used as construction materials for thousands of years. With interest in sustainable or 'green' building solutions, bricks fabricated by mushroom mycelia deserve further study and investment.

Mushrooms for sale in a Paris market.

Black morel, *Morchella conica*.

*twelve*

# Mushroom Cooking

Mushrooms have enthralled gourmets for millennia by adding unique flavours, aromas and textures to recipes. A nondescript risotto is transformed into a celebration of life with a handful of porcini; cream of chanterelle soup has been described as 'sex in a bowl', and the glistening gills of meadow mushroom caps make a fried breakfast the highlight of a weekend.[1] Against this bacchanalia, the truth about mushrooms is that their tastes are often overrated and they have very little nutritional value. This chapter puts mushrooms in their proper place in our diet.

In the eastern United States, morels attract a lot of attention from food writers and are a welcome sign of spring after a gruelling winter. Weekend forays encourage thousands of enthusiasts to pick fruit bodies of yellow morels (*Morchella esculenta*), black morels (*Morchella elata*) and other species of these ascomycete mushrooms with dimpled heads. Fresh morels sautéed in cream and eaten on toast are delicious. They have an earthy flavour and nutty texture, but the principal aftertaste of the dish comes from the rich cream. The protein and fat content of the dish are similarly dominated by the cream. Morels, like other mushrooms, have few calories and claims about the importance of the antioxidants in their flesh have no basis in reality.

If morels are replaced by white button mushrooms from a supermarket, the loss of flavour is not as great as morel enthusiasts imagine. A blind taste test with buttons competing against morels would be revealing, but I think that my case is convincing without it. Sliced button mushrooms cooked in butter are delicious; they are a wonderful accompaniment to fried eggs. Like morels, however, button mushrooms are relished, in part, because butter is such delectable stuff. If readers doubt the truth of this somewhat dampening evaluation of mushrooms, consider eating them sliced raw in a salad. Their blandness is undeniable. Other ingredients offer fabulous stand-alone flavours. Fresh summer tomatoes, onions, radishes and cucumbers have their own personalities. Most mushrooms are a bit of a let-down. Morels should not be eaten raw anyway; some people are sickened by an unknown component in these fungi that is nullified by cooking.

The mushroom smell is immediately recognizable. It is conveyed by a chemical called octenol, or 1-octen-3-ol, more memorable as 'mushroom alcohol'. The same compound is found in human breath and sweat, but at levels sufficiently low that we smell of things other than mushrooms. When young puffballs are diced, the release of mushroom alcohol accounts for the similarity in their fragrance to fresh button mushrooms. The puffball has an additional bouquet, but it is very difficult to tell puffballs apart from button mushrooms when they are cooked in butter or olive oil. Giant puffballs do not have much personality either. Round slabs of their white flesh hold up to the heat of an outdoor grill, but adopt the flavour of a glaze or marinade rather than delivering their own taste. Oil and garlic work well with these generous servings of mushroom steak. A drizzle of balsamic vinegar and a few sprigs of rosemary are also recommended by many cooks. And this is the essence of most mushroom recipes: fruit bodies are used for their texture and appearance, and serve as carriers for other flavours in the dish.

The popular cultivated mushrooms do not taste very strongly of anything, but they certainly add texture and enliven the appearance of a dish with their curious shapes. Consider the appeal of stir-fried onions, carrots and green beans, before and after the addition of a handful of enokitake mushrooms. The etiolated fruit bodies of enokitake are instantly forgettable for their flavour (raw ones have less taste that wet paper), but they are a welcome surprise among sliced vegetables in a sweet and sour sauce served over steaming rice. Oyster mushrooms are in the same 'nice to look at' category.

Shiitake often moves from dullness to unpleasantness, but is excused by food critics who feel compelled to say something in favour of this rather rubbery fruit body. These mushrooms can convey a certain woodiness, but I doubt that the Romans would have had anything to do with them. After all, in the nineteenth century it was alleged by the *Ispettore dei Funghi* – the official who policed mushroom markets in Rome – that he had been directed by the government to ensure that any meadow mushrooms detected in sellers' baskets were thrown into the Tiber along with maggot-ridden or poisonous fruit bodies.[2] This may be an exaggerated story derived from the high regard paid to other species by Italian cooks. Meadow mushrooms were certainly eaten in ancient Rome. Ovid describes a countrywoman in his *Fasti*, or *Book of Days*, gathering *fungos albos*, white mushrooms, which must be a reference to *Agaricus campestris*.[3]

Roman chefs knew a lot about mushrooms, according highest praise for Caesar's mushroom, *Amanita caesarea*. This species was so venerated in the Roman kitchen that special baking dishes called *boletaria* were made for warming the fruit bodies. The northern distribution of the species along Roman roads in Switzerland suggests

Slabs of giant puffball, *Calvatia gigantea*, prepared for grilling.

that its spores may have been spread by soldiers who carried the fruit bodies on their marches. Roman chefs served Caesar's mushrooms raw as the star in a simple salad dressed with olive oil, lemon and salt. This dish has survived for more than two thousand years. Fruit bodies are picked in the egg stage, or in the early stages of emergence from their eggs, and are called *ovoli* (meaning eggs) in Italian cuisine.

*Lactarius deliciosus* and other milkcaps were also enjoyed by Romans and remain popular today. Fruit bodies in a fresco uncovered at Herculaneum look like milkcaps. There is a theme in this historical and ongoing ranking of edible mushrooms: the most flavourful species are mycorrhizal. Fungi raised on manure or logs tend to be quite characterless by comparison. Mushroom enthusiasts can verify this by thinking about species they have eaten. Fruit bodies of *Boletus edulis*, or porcini, are delicious fresh or dried. Dried porcini keep for ages and provide depth and a rich smokiness to soups and stews. Porcini are the only mushrooms that encourage me to draw upon the more extravagant terms used to describe wines, like saddle leather and melting road tar, but I will limit myself to suggesting that this mushroom has a wonderful

Eggs of Caesar's mushroom, *Amanita caesarea*, in an Italian market.

earthy fragrance, redolent of the rich soil around an ancient oak tree. (This is not much of a stretch, because porcini often grow beneath oaks.) Chanterelles are described by their fans as meaty and aromatic. They are mycorrhizal too.

The contrast with wild saprotrophs is striking. Chicken-of-the-woods, *Laetiporus sulphureus*, is a radiant yellow-orange bracket fungus, but its taste is indistinct. It is a wood-decay mushroom that grows on logs. Other fungi that decompose wood have a stronger taste, but this is not necessarily a good thing. Many years ago I cooked a fresh bracket of dryad's saddle, *Polyporus squamosus*, using an elaborate recipe that called for saffron, garlic and a dozen other herbs and spices. The taste of the resulting stew is difficult to describe accurately, but might be revisited (at least in one's imagination) by simmering lumps of pork fat in cologne, with added flakes of mortuary soap for frothiness. Twenty years have passed since this abomination bubbled away in my kitchen and the memory still leaves me queasy. The mushroom must have absorbed some of the resinous flavour of the rotting tree stump on which it grew before decapitation. It took revenge on its executioner in the

Dryad's saddle, *Polyporus squamosus*, growing on a tree stump.

133

kitchen. An exorcist confronted with this brew would have cast their phial of holy water towards the pot, yelled, 'Get thee behind me!' and flown through the door. You will find recipes for dryad's saddle on the Internet. Do not trust them.

Something about the mycorrhizal connection makes all the difference when it comes to taste. The provision of food to the mushroom mycelium by its plant partners is part of the story. Sugars are accompanied by other compounds when they are transferred from the plant to the fungus, and the mycelium may be generating its own aromatic molecules to tighten its bonds with the plant. The case for mycorrhizal superiority is settled by ascomycete truffles, which partner with oaks and whose exotic taste goes beyond the fleshly delights of any gilled mushroom.[4] Truffle flavours evolved as animal attractants and can prove overwhelming for the uninitiated diner (who should pass them to me). Spectroscopic analysis of the gases wafting from white truffles identified more than one hundred volatile compounds, including aromatic hydrocarbons, phenols and sulphurous chemicals. Truffle lovers are suffused with sensational tastes. The false truffles among the basidiomycetes may have some interesting flavours, but their edibility has not been tested. This task falls to a twenty-first-century Captain McIlvaine.

The nutritional value of mushrooms lies in their lack of calories. It is impossible to get fat eating raw mushrooms. This seems surprising, perhaps, when we think about a fruit body that feels as firm as a chicken nugget, but the caloric density of these foods is very different. A chicken nugget that weighs 20 g contains almost sixty calories or 250 kilojoules. Sixty per cent of the energy in this battered meat product (battered applying to every stage of nugget manufacture) lies in its fat. The same weight of fresh mushrooms packs only four calories, which is one calorie higher than an equivalent serving of lettuce. If mushrooms are eaten raw, they are great for weight loss. If they are cooked in a knob of butter containing three times more calories than a chicken nugget, all bets are off.

The difference in caloric density of mushrooms versus chicken is due to the preponderance of water and indigestible fibre in the fungus. Up to 90 per cent of a fresh mushroom can be water. This is evident from the process of mushroom expansion, which involves the absorption of water rather than the formation of lots of new tissue. Raw mushrooms contain a pinch of digestible carbohydrate, a trace of fat and a whiff of vitamins. One could obtain greater sustenance by licking a postage stamp. This makes sense from the 'viewpoint' of the mycelium. Fungi, like all organisms, are going to use the bare minimum of resources to construct their reproductive organs. Any materials that are not essential for producing and releasing spores are wasteful. Fungi have an additional reason for keeping their mushrooms lean. Any increase in calorific value will increase the attractiveness of the fruit body to animals, so making a mushroom that offers little sustenance to woodland creatures is a very good idea. There are limits to this economy, which probably explains why some fungi invest in the protection afforded by toxins. Fungi whose spores are dispersed by animals are an obvious exception to these evolutionary strategies. False truffles, for example, grow with the explicit purpose of attracting rodents to spread their spores.

Self-proclaimed experts in human nutrition make extraordinary declarations about the dietary value of mushrooms, but most of their advice is founded on pseudoscience, wishful thinking and plain silliness. There is a strain of desperation in their proclamations when they resort to the idea that the importance of mushrooms lies in their potassium content. It is quite difficult to suffer from low potassium if one consumes anything approaching a normal diet. 'Authorities' on the miraculous nutritional properties of mushrooms muddy the discussion further when they summon the phantom of antioxidants and other supposedly healthy properties of fungi. My scepticism runneth over whenever the science of mycology is co-opted by people who have not made the effort to think objectively about the real virtues of mushrooms. And there is so much that is inspiring about the truth of mushroom biology that has been learned from experiments. There is more than enough to engage an enquiring mind for decades and, sweeping aside the fairy tales, there is a lifetime of enjoyment in identifying, cooking and eating wild mushrooms. There is no need to decorate the splendid truth.

# *thirteen*
# Mushroom Poisons

Emperor Claudius loved the eponymous Caesar's mushroom, *Amanita caesarea*, providing the opportunity for his wife, Agrippina, to dispatch him by substituting similar-looking death caps, *Amanita phalloides*, in his favourite dish. The story is recalled in Juvenal's *Satires*, when the narrator suggests that lowly guests at a banquet can be served mushrooms of dubious provenance, but 'for my lord, a rare mushroom, the kind that Claudius guzzled (until his wife fed him one that wrote finis to his eating)'.[1] Juvenal uses the word *boletus* for this rare mushroom, which has confused historians unfamiliar with the Roman use of *boleti* to refer to fruit bodies of Caesar's mushroom rather than porcini. The unrelated porcini were given the Latin name *Boletus edulis* in the eighteenth century. If this brown-capped mushroom had been the species that Claudius thought he was guzzling, he would surely have noticed the substitution of death caps, and Agrippina's assassination attempt would have failed. I hope this tortuous explanation makes sense and that this soupçon of mycological history is settled forever.

The story may, in fact, be fictitious. After two thousand years, it is impossible to be sure that Emperor Claudius was murdered with any kind of mushroom. Writing a few months after the emperor's death in AD 54, Seneca reported that his last words were, 'Oh my! I think I have shit myself,' which does not square with the classic symptoms of a lingering death associated with death caps.[2] Accounts are complicated by later references to mushrooms to which poison had been added, rather than innately poisonous mushrooms, and even to a poison administered to the emperor on a feather used under the pretence of clearing his throat.

One of the white *Amanita* species, called 'destroying angels'.

Death caps can take more than a week to kill their victims. The first phase of the poisoning occurs in the first few hours after eating the fruit bodies and takes the form of severe gastrointestinal distress. Claudius was in poor health before his exit, so it is possible that this was enough to dispatch him. More often, victims who are rehydrated after this unpleasantness experience a latent or honeymoon period for a few days before the signs of liver and kidney damage become apparent. The honeymoon phase is disastrous, because the casualty is unaware of the damage being done by the mushroom toxins and does not seek treatment.[3]

Death caps and the related destroying angels contain a toxin called alpha-amanitin. There is enough of this substance in a single fruit body to provide a lethal dose for an adult, and half a mushroom will kill a child. Amanitin works by inhibiting an enzyme that is crucial for producing proteins in our cells and wrecks the liver when it is absorbed into the bloodstream from the gut. If the poisoning is detected shortly after eating the mushroom, stomach pumping (gastric lavage) can prevent the absorption of the amanitin. Once the fruit body tissue passes into the gut, however, treatment options are limited. Fluid replacement and other forms of supportive care are essential to keep the patient alive, but after a few days, liver transplantation is the only recourse in the severest poisoning cases. There are no effective drug therapies at the moment, though the protective effect of a compound called silibinin against liver damage is under investigation. Silibinin is extracted from milk thistle seeds. In other clinical studies, the toxicity of alpha-amanitin is being exploited by linking it to an antibody to target and destroy cancer cells.

Most cases of alpha-amanitin poisoning are thought to be due to similarities in the appearance of toxic species of *Amanita* and cultivated or wild edible mushrooms. The popularity of the culti- vated paddy straw mushroom, *Volvariella volvacea*, in Asian cuisine presents a danger for immigrants who settle in the Western hemisphere. It can be difficult to tell fruit bodies of the paddy straw mushroom apart from the destroying angels – *Amanita*

Deadly galerina, *Galerina marginata*, fruiting on a wet log.

*bisporigera* and *Amanita ocreata* in North America and *Amanita virosa* in Europe – especially when they are young. Mature fruit bodies of the paddy straw mushroom are pink, distinguishing this species from the poisonous white-gilled species of *Amanita*. The yellow egg mushroom, *Amanita princeps*, sold in markets in Southeast Asia, is another edible lookalike that may confuse immigrants who come across toxic amanitas in North America.[4] This could be a greater threat than that posed by the cultivated paddy straw mushroom because it is a wild species picked in forests, which the Hmong and other ethnic groups are used to finding in their homelands.

Appreciable levels of alpha-amanitin also occur in mushrooms outside the amanita family, including *Galerina marginata* and *Conocybe filaris*. *Galerina* is a small mushroom with brown caps that fruits in clusters on rotting logs. It is a typical 'little brown mushroom', which does not tend to attract much attention from pickers. This is a good thing given that its common name is deadly galerina. Poisonings by this mushroom are exceedingly rare and would not occur at all if people were more cautious in their pursuit of small brownish mushrooms containing hallucinogens.

Deadly poisonous fool's webcap, *Cortinarius orellanus*.

*Conocybe* is another relatively inconspicuous mushroom that contains the same toxin, grows on lawns and might be mistaken for a magic mushroom by a naive picker.

Poisonous webcaps contain another toxin called orellanine. These species of *Cortinarius* are as dangerous as death caps and destroying angels. Some chanterelle species look similar to the poisonous webcaps, though most victims of *Cortinarius* poisoning are probably looking for hallucinogenic *Psilocybe* mushrooms. *Cortinarius orellanus*, the fool's webcap, and *Cortinarius rubellus*, the deadly webcap, are the commonest fungi implicated in orellanine poisoning, but other species contain the same toxin. Orellanine has a similar chemical structure to the herbicides paraquat and diquat. It disrupts cells in the kidney tubules and leads to kidney failure. Unfortunate victims are prone to dismiss the relationship between the first symptoms of nausea and vomiting and eating mushrooms, because they can be delayed for a few days after the meal. Like the latent phase of death cap poisoning, this slow unfolding of symptoms limits treatment options. More specific indications, of extreme thirst, frequent urination and kidney pain, come later and patients can die without dialysis. Kidney transplantation offers the best outcome in the most serious cases.

Poisonings by other kinds of mushroom toxins are associated with very different symptoms.[5] Yellow fruit bodies of man-on-horseback, *Tricholoma equestre*, are identified as popular edibles in many field guides, but have caused some spectacular poisonings. The toxins in this fungus, which have not been identified, destroy muscle tissue and lead to breathing difficulties, kidney damage and cardiovascular collapse. Given the long tradition of eating this mushroom in Europe, the small number of poisonings are perplexing. In a cluster of cases in Bordeaux, investigators found that the patients had eaten man-on-horseback fruit bodies in three consecutive meals before symptoms of muscle weakness began. Repeated exposure to the same toxin seems to be the obvious mechanism at work here. Another possibility is that high levels of these noxious compounds are generated by mycelia of *Tricholoma equestre* in particular areas in response to unusual environmental conditions. This is alarming for pickers who have no way of knowing which fruit bodies are safe. Another poisonous mushroom called *Russula subnigricans* can also cause muscle damage. Victims are struck with speech impairment and convulsions a few minutes after eating this fungus and fatalities have been reported in Japan.

The harmful effects of the common ink cap, *Coprinopsis atramentaria*, are experienced when the mushroom meal is washed down with alcohol (see page 11). A compound called coprine produced by this fungus blocks ethanol metabolism so that the unfortunate diner is treated to an appalling hangover that can be misdiagnosed as alcohol poisoning. The false morel, *Gyromitra esculenta*, contains a chemical called gyromitrin that is converted into monomethylhydrazine (MMH) after the mushroom is ingested. The same chemical is manufactured for use as a rocket propellant. The toxin from the mushroom causes nausea and vomiting and can lead to liver and kidney damage. In the most severe cases, people have experienced seizures and died after becoming comatose. Undeterred by these possibilities, false morel fanatics parboil the fruit bodies to get rid of the toxin. It must be a really tasty mushroom to take this risk.

The reason that death caps, webcaps and other mushrooms produce toxins is a mystery. Because humans and other apes evolved so recently in relation to fungi, we cannot be the intended targets of these chemical weapons. Mushroom toxins are more likely designed, in an evolutionary sense, to combat the development of larvae that hatch from eggs laid by insects and worms in the fruit body tissues. The number of truly dangerous mushrooms is very small. Only a hundred or so types of mushroom, or less than 1 per cent of the known species, have been associated with poisonings. This compares favourably with the estimated six hundred species of venomous snake, which represent 20 per cent of the total number of these animals. On a less positive note, antivenoms offer antidotes

Frontispiece from an 18th-century book on mushroom identification by Giovanni Antonio Battarra. The translated banner reads, 'We look at mushrooms but do not eat them.' The owl and the lynx symbolize sharp senses.

to the most common snakebites, whereas there are no cures for the worst kinds of mushroom poisoning.

Spoilage of edible mushrooms collected in warm weather and kept in plastic bags is probably a more common cause of intestinal distress than eating poisonous fungi. This more generalized food poisoning does not garner much attention compared with the drama of death caps. News stories about mushroom poisonings have a big shock factor, particularly when an entire family is wasted by an error in identification. The first books about mushrooms sought to document the range of fungi while pointing out the species that should be avoided. The lovely frontispiece of Battarra's *Fungorum agri ariminenesis historia*, published in 1755, provided an explicit warning about death caps. A lynx is pawing a death cap below a banner that reads, 'We look at mushrooms but do not eat them.' This recommendation was not applied to all mushrooms, because an owl perched next to the lynx is surrounded by a harvest of edible fungi, including a morel. Battarra's use of the lynx was a nod towards the Accademia dei Lincei, or Academy of the Lynx-eyed, the famous scientific society founded in Italy in 1603.

Mushroom on the cover of a creationist book that depicts biologists as a poisonous influence on society.

Mushroom toxicity remains a source of superstitions about fungi and is at the root of the way many people treat the discovery of a fruit body on a lawn or beside a woodland trail: by kicking it. This almost unconscious act demolishes a miracle of evolutionary engineering. D. H. Lawrence used mushrooms as a symbol of human corruption in the following excerpts from his poem 'How Beastly the Bourgeois Is':

> Nicely groomed, like a mushroom
> standing there so sleek and erect and eyeable –
> and like a fungus, living on the remains
>     of a bygone life
> sucking his life out of the dead leaves of greater life
>     than his own.
>
>     . . .

Standing in their thousands, these appearances, in
    damp England
what a pity they can't all be kicked over
like sickening toadstools, and left to melt back, swiftly
into the soil of England.[6]

My love of mushrooms is a source of considerable bias here, but this poem diminishes my respect for D. H. Lawrence. It takes greater sensitivity to nature to go beyond these stereotypes and appreciate the beauty of mushrooms and their importance in supporting the health of the planet. They sustain forests by 'sucking life out of dead leaves', as Lawrence had it, and thereby make things habitable for us. Let it become known that anyone who kicks mushrooms displays their ignorance of the nature of life and death. The goblins will get them in the end.

Mushrooms were misrepresented in European fairy tales too, and their long-standing vilification was exploited by Nazi propagandists. In a children's book called *Der Giftpilz*, meaning 'The Toadstool', young readers were warned about Jews through a conversation between a mother and son who are foraging in the woods:

Look, Franz, human beings in this world are like the mushrooms in the forest. There are good mushrooms and there are good people. There are poisonous, bad mushrooms and there are bad people. And we have to be on our guard against bad people just as we have to be on guard against poisonous mushrooms. Do you understand that?[7]

In an act of lesser evil, but equivalent idiocy, an American creationist used mushrooms in a cartoon as a symbol for the pernicious influence of science teachers upon society. This illustration was published in the 1920s, long before genetic studies demonstrated the unity of all living things and the shared evolutionary history of fungi and creationists.

# fourteen
# Mushroom Medicines

Mushrooms have featured in traditional Chinese medicine for centuries and dried extracts from fruit bodies occupy a lucrative segment of the market for herbal medicines in Western countries. The advertising of these natural products in North America and Europe is poorly regulated, allowing companies to make fictitious claims about the medicinal benefits of mushrooms. A number of issues must be considered objectively to assess this controversial topic. We begin with the traditional uses of mushroom remedies in Chinese medicine.[1]

Medicinal use of the shiitake mushroom, *Lentinula edodes*, became widespread in the Ming dynasty (1368–1644) after the development of methods for cultivating the fungus on logs.[2] Shiitake was adopted as a tonic that could counteract the quotidian aches, pains and fatigue associated with ageing. More specific virtues of shiitake were supposed to include its promotion of heart health and efficacy against lung disease and intestinal worms. It also became associated with the treatment of cancer. There is little experimental support for any of these qualities, but today's advocates of medicinal mushrooms suggest that this dissonance is due to the mismatch in philosophy between Chinese and Western medicine.

Traditional Chinese medicine treats symptoms of cardiovascular disease, for example, as a manifestation of an imbalance between multiple physiological processes in an individual patient. Treatments, including acupuncture and herbal medicines, are designed to restore balance to the 'flow of energy' in the body. ('Flow of energy' is placed in quotation marks because the meaning of this phrase cannot be articulated in any succinct manner.)

Western medicine addresses some forms of heart disease very differently, by prescribing drugs that reduce blood pressure or serum cholesterol, and recommending changes in diet and exercise. The use of a combination of therapies in Chinese medicine, which is often adjusted for individuals, makes it difficult to assess the particular usefulness of shiitake mushrooms in a clinical trial.

A handful of experiments on the properties of specific chemical compounds extracted from shiitake have been promising.[3] Lentinan is a big molecule in the cell walls that wrap around the masses of hyphal filaments that form the shiitake fruit body. It is a polysaccharide made from long, branching chains of sugar molecules twisted into thicker cables. Lentinan research has demonstrated that the molecule acts as an adjuvant, stimulating the production of antibodies in mice injected with a vaccine against hepatitis B. Other experiments on tissue cultures show that lentinan stimulates the immune system to attack cancer cells and cells infected with viruses. In a rare instance of a clinical trial using a mushroom extract, Japanese researchers found that patients receiving chemotherapy for advanced stomach cancer survived longer if lentinan was added to their drug cocktail. These results fall short of proving that shiitake is useful in cancer therapy, but they should certainly encourage further study.

Experiments showing that cell wall components from mushrooms have stimulatory effects upon the immune system appear, at first glance, to buttress the historical case for using mushrooms, but there is reason for caution. One of the problems is that the results of investigations on single chemical compounds may not apply to the consumption of whole fruit bodies or concoctions made from dried mushroom powder. Similarly, studies in which cell wall preparations are injected into the bloodstream of mice are difficult to relate to the effects of drinking hot tea brewed from shiitake. Nevertheless, companies that market medicinal products exploit the insubstantial relationship between the studies on mice and mushroom extracts that are sold in capsules and throat sprays. They also base their trade on the bromide of special knowledge privileged to Asian cultures. It is instructive to consider that life expectancy in China has increased from 35 years in the 1940s to 75 today. Many factors contributed to this phenomenal demographic change, but the introduction of Western medicine is significant.[4] Most Chinese people choose modern medicine when they have a serious illness.

As the Chinese embrace Western medicine, the global appetite for herbal supplements has moved in the opposite direction. Annual sales of these products account for a substantial chunk of the market for nutritional supplements, which is valued at $50 billion and seems impervious to the economic instability that has affected other business sectors.[5] This lucrative industry provides a powerful incentive for companies to test the credulity of their customers and unsupported assertions have come to define the medicinal mushroom business.

Lingzhi or reishi, *Ganoderma lucidum*, cultivated on bags filled with sawdust.

Hardened sclerotium
of chaga, *Inonotus
obliquus*.

The bracket fungus *Ganoderma lucidum*, called lingzhi in
China and reishi in Japan, is one of the most popular medicinal
mushrooms and has a history of use in China that is even older
than that of shiitake. Lingzhi is mentioned in a two-thousand-
year-old poem from the Han dynasty and earlier descriptions of
the 'Mushroom of Immortality' probably refer to this species.
The fungus grows on rotting wood in the wild and is cultivated
on sawdust or straw packed into plastic bags. A short stalk supports the kidney-shaped bracket of this species, which releases
spores from tiny pores that perforate its white underbelly. The
rest of the fruit body surface develops a brittle shell with a glossy
red-orange colour. It looks as if it has been lacquered with a thick
coat of paint. Like shiitake, lingzhi is believed to have an immense
range of benefits and is used to treat cancer, seizures, cardiovascular problems, diabetes and many other ailments. Comprehensive
reviews of the available evidence dampen enthusiasm for lingzhi,
offering no support for the use of this mushroom in treating heart
disease or cancer.[6] Investigators reached the same conclusions
in their evaluation of the extensive studies on the little bracket
fungus *Trametes versicolor*, or turkey tail.[7]

Maitake, *Grifola frondosa*, for sale in a market.

Chaga, *Inonotus obliquus*, grows as a rock-hard excrescence from birch trees. This dense structure does not produce spores but is constructed in the same way as a fruit body, from a mass of filamentous hyphae. It is called a sclerotium. The powdered sclerotia of chaga have been used as a folk remedy against cancer, and the fungus features in Aleksandr Solzhenitsyn's brilliant and disturbing novel *Cancer Ward* (1968).[8] Reviewing experiments showing the effects of chaga extracts on cultured cells, the Memorial Sloan Kettering Cancer Center in New York concluded, 'No clinical trials have been conducted to assess chaga's safety and efficacy for disease prevention or for the treatment of cancer, cardiovascular disease, or diabetes.'[9] Much the same applies to maitake, *Grifola frondosa*, also known as hen-of-the-woods, which is a polypore that grows as masses of fruit bodies at the base of oak trees.[10] The only thing that we can say with confidence is that extracts from shiitake, lingzhi, turkey tail, chaga and maitake stimulate cells of the immune system in tissue culture experiments. With so little critical study of the benefits of medicinal mushrooms, it is alarming that the potential harm done by these natural products has been neglected. A few studies suggest that any side effects of mushroom extracts are not serious, but cases of food allergy, cheilitis (inflammation of the lips), flagellate erythema and liver damage have been reported.[11]

The medicinal mushroom product range of a major supplier in the United States includes a variety of capsules and bottled fluids that contain extracts from cultured mushroom mycelia. 'Healthy respiratory support' is furnished by a mixture of reishi and other mushrooms; chaga extract deals with 'antioxidant and DNA support'; and maitake offers the promise of helping to 'maintain healthy blood sugar levels.'[12] Another group of products targets particular parts of the body, with one dietary supplement addressing 'breast health', another covering the brain ('helps to support mental clarity') and a third dealing with the liver. The list of ingredients of these supplements includes mushrooms that support immune function (turkey tail) and hormonal and adrenal function (lingzhi). An asterisk accompanies every medicinal property, referencing the following manufacturer's disclaimer: 'These statements have not been evaluated by the Food and Drug Administration. This product is not intended to diagnose, treat, cure or prevent any disease.' This is like making bicycles and telling customers that they are not meant to be ridden!

Surprisingly, these product claims are quite modest compared with endorsements provided by other peddlers of naturopathic medicines. If something is sold for the purpose of improving heart health, it seems reasonable that there should be some evidence for its effectiveness and that this information should be available to the consumer. Unlike prescription drugs, medicinal mushrooms have escaped these requirements, which means that a mushroom extract can be sold in the United States for the stated purpose of supporting 'comprehensive immune support', or just about anything else, as long as the company provides the standard disclaimer. The laws in Europe are even looser, allowing companies in the United Kingdom to market medicinal mushrooms without employing a legal rider. The medicinal mushroom industry is aware of growing criticism of its practices and many companies have scaled back their advertising to avoid legal repercussions. Until quite recently, some catalogues listed extracts from cultures of mushroom mycelia for the treatment of particular kinds of cancer and other serious diseases. Few companies make these claims directly today, even under the protection of the asterisk.

Most prescription medicines work by affecting particular biochemical pathways. The best-selling drugs for reducing cholesterol levels and blood pressure inhibit single enzymes, and antibiotics disrupt specific molecular processes in bacterial cells. None of these medicines are perfect and all of them can produce unpleasant side effects. But most of them work as advertised and the manufacturers can be held liable if their products harm consumers. Horrifying errors have been made in licensing some medicines, and the pharmaceuticals industry wins few awards for altruism but – warts and all – prescription drugs are a perfect reflection of the ethos of Western medicine. Anyone whose life has been saved by antibiotic therapy is likely to agree that these compounds are the miracle drugs of the twentieth century.

Pursuing this critical exploration of medicinal mushrooms, it seems very likely that mushrooms *do* contain compounds with important pharmacological properties. This optimism is encouraged by the deep biological history of interactions between fruit bodies and animals. The ability of mushrooms to survive damage by insects and other pests long enough to release spores suggests that they generate a range of cryptic antifeedant chemicals that interact with molecular targets in animals. Toxins and hallucinogenic compounds synthesized by fruit bodies are obvious examples of mushroom products with extraordinary pharmacological activities. Disregarding the dafter ideas about medicinal mushrooms, it is possible that these fungi offer a treasure trove of uncharacterized metabolites that could prove useful in treating our illnesses.

Lion's mane, *Hericium erinaceus*, cultivated on bags of sawdust and woodchips.

The work on ubiquitous compounds like lentinan from shiitake may be a distraction from more productive lines of inquiry. Lentinan is a version of a polysaccharide that is found in all fungi. These polysaccharides are called beta-glucans. Although it is possible that there is something special about the chemical structure of lentinan, cell wall materials extracted from any mushroom are likely to have the same medicinal properties as lentinan. Shiitake may have been adopted in China for the simple reason that it was easy to grow. A better model for future research on medicinal mushrooms is provided by a pair of molecules identified in *Hericium erinaceus*, or lion's mane. This is another mushroom that has been used in China for centuries. Its common name refers to the resemblance between the long spines of the fruit body and the luxuriant hair surrounding the face of a male lion. Like lingzhi, it is cultivated on sawdust pellets. This species has become associated with the unusual characteristic of promoting neurological health, which attracts a lot of attention in a time of ageing human populations and the spectre of Alzheimer's disease. The active compounds extracted from lion's mane are called erinacines and hericenones. Erinacines and hericenones stimulate the release of nerve growth factor in rat brains and cultured nerve cells.[13] This effect seems worthy of additional analysis.

The worst of the advertisements for medicinal mushrooms recall the era of medical quackery that tolerated patent medicines, such as 'Dr Bonker's Celebrated Egyptian Oil', which was advertised as a cure for colic and cramps in humans *and* farm animals, and 'Dr Solomon's Cordial Balm of Gilead', which was supposedly effective against venereal disease and just about every other malady.[14] Putting aside the current fantasies about mushrooms, there are good reasons for surveying the galaxy of metabolites in these organisms. After all, other kinds of fungi are the source of antibiotics old (penicillin) and new (cephalosporins), the cholesterol-lowering drug lovastatin, and cyclosporines for supporting patients after organ transplants.[15] Miraculous drugs could be sitting in the least prepossessing fruit bodies. And with a choice of sixteen thousand or more species of basidiomycetes that form mushrooms, there are lots of places to look. It is time to treat anti-ageing tonics made from mushrooms as a sad phase in the history of mycology and proceed with the exploration of novel compounds with the potential to change the course of our modern plagues.

# fifteen
# Mushroom Hallucinogens

This mycological topic is approached with some misgiving by the author, who has invested a little more than thirty years in the study of fungi without experiencing the effects of magic mushrooms. My sole defence, when questioned by people who have enjoyed the neurological festivities stimulated by psilocybes, is that they have not been party to the psychiatric journeys of my life. There is more than enough going on in my circuitry without the addition of a handful of dried mushrooms. Life unaltered is curious enough for some. Even for the inexperienced, however, there is a great deal to be learned from considering the neurotropic effects of the metabolites in these fungi.

Psilocybin is regarded as the most potent of the hallucinogenic compounds produced by mushrooms. It is found in the gilled fruit bodies of more than two hundred species of *Psilocybe*, *Panaeolus*, *Conocybe*, *Galerina* and other genera. More than half of magic mushrooms are *Psilocybe* species.[1] The mycelia of these fungi grow in meadows and in forests, feeding as saprotrophs on decomposing plants. A few species fruit on herbivore dung or from soil enriched by this natural fertilizer. *Psilocybe semilanceata*, the liberty cap, is a common grassland mushroom in Europe that is picked from the wild. *Psilocybe cubensis* is a subtropical mushroom that is the commonest cultivated source of psilocybin. Its spores are sold in syringes and it is quite easy to grow on rice flour and other grains. This is illegal in most countries and there are severe penalties for those caught trading the mushrooms. Nevertheless, sales of spores and dried psilocybes represent a thriving underground business. Some companies sell materials used for culturing magic mushrooms by offering their

Magic mushrooms, *Psilocybe cubensis*, in their natural habitat.

products for growing *any* kind of mushroom. Where there's a will, there's a way.

After mushroom ingestion, psilocybin is converted into psilocin, the psychoactive compound.[2] The structure of the psilocin molecule is very similar to serotonin, allowing it to interfere with a range of neurological processes by binding to serotonin receptors in the brain. These receptors affect the release of dopamine and other neurotransmitter molecules that convey signals across

Liberty caps, *Psilocybe semilanceata.*

synaptic connections. Neuroimaging studies on patients given purified psilocybin reveal changes in blood flow associated with a decrease in neurological activity in multiple regions of the brain.[3] The overall reduction in blood flow is similar to the change in brain activity observed during sleep, which may account for the frequent descriptions of dreamlike experiences under the influence of magic mushrooms. Psilocybin also enhances communication between parts of the brain that are isolated during normal neurological function. This is called synaesthesia and probably explains the perception of colours as sounds and vice versa. Changes in the awareness of oneself and the passage of time are other common experiences. Few people are frightened by these experiences in supportive settings, either among friends or during a controlled clinical experiment, and most say they feel elevated. This has encouraged interest in using psilocybin to treat clinical depression and to reduce anxiety in patients with a terminal illness.

The effects of magic mushrooms were probably familiar to people thousands of years ago, but most of the claims about ancient rituals involving mushrooms are not supported by critical archaeological and anthropological research. Mushrooms appear in prehistoric petroglyphs in the Tassili n'Ajjer mountains in Algeria. This site, deep in the Sahara Desert, was a productive savannah in the Neolithic when the rock carvings were made. One of the petroglyphs shows 'mushroom men' holding fruit bodies as they run across the scene; another shows an imposing figure clutching fistfuls of mushrooms with fruit bodies sprouting all over its body.[4] Mushrooms are also depicted in Neolithic cave paintings in Spain, but we have no idea what symbolic role they held for the artists.[5]

Mushrooms have been spotted as more recent stand-ins for the tree of knowledge in medieval European artworks, including an illuminated manuscript and a wall painting in a French chapel. The 'trees' in these sources have the shape of a mushroom, but umbrella pines and various fruit trees are represented in a similar, albeit less ambiguous, fashion in other medieval artworks. The famous thirteenth-century fresco of the tree of knowledge in Plaincourault Chapel in France, for example, looks more like one of these stylized plants than a stem bearing multiple mushrooms.[6] Any extension of these observations to theories about

Neolithic rock carvings at Tassili n'Ajjer in the Algerian part of the Sahara Desert. Some authors have interpreted the figures as dancers carrying mushrooms.

Digital tracing of the Selva Pascal mural, a work of prehistoric rock art from Cuenca in Spain, showing pictographs that resemble mushrooms.

the worship of hallucinogenic mushrooms by early Christians are baseless. A better case could be made for the significance of a psychotropic drug made by a microscopic fungus in the origin of Christianity itself: alcohol, produced by the single-celled yeast *Saccharomyces cerevisiae*, has powerful effects upon cognition and plays an important role in the faith. The transformation of water into wine was the first miracle performed by Jesus, and for the Catholic faithful, wine becomes the blood of Christ in the Communion.

The clearest instance of the use of magic mushrooms in religious rituals comes from descriptions of the Aztec culture in which the fruit bodies were regarded as the flesh of the gods, or *teonanácatl*, and permitted communication between the gods and their priests.[7] The purported discovery of the continuing worship of psilocybes in Mexico in the 1950s was based on work of doubtful reliability. Gordon Wasson, an investment banker who invested his personal fortune in this investigation, appears to have been fooled by a woman who conducted ceremonies with psilocybes that involved hours of meaningless chanting. Albert Hoffmann, the chemist who manufactured LSD, was responsible for identifying psilocybin as the psychoactive compound in

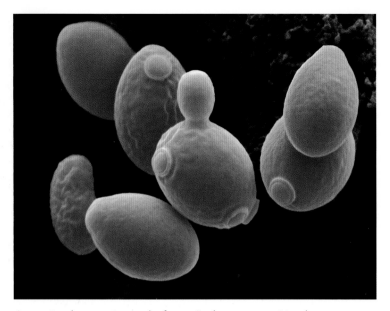

A scanning electron micrograph of yeast, *Saccharomyces cerevisiae*, the most important psychotropic fungus.

cultures grown from mushrooms collected by Wasson and botanist Roger Heim in Mexico.

Long before Wasson's investigations in Mexico, reports of the use of mushrooms as intoxicants came from explorers in the Russian Far East. The chain of custody for these intriguing stories stretches back to the Swedish cartographer Philip Johan von Strahlenberg, who travelled in Siberia and on the Kamchatka Peninsula in the early eighteenth century. Von Strahlenberg reported that the indigenous Koryak people traded animal furs for a particular kind of mushroom, boiled the fruit bodies in water and become inebriated when they drank the liquor.[8] Poorer people without their own store of mushrooms enjoyed similar effects by drinking their richer neighbours' urine. This delicate cultural transaction involved the capture of urine in wooden bowls after a mushroom feast.

Petroglyphs from Siberia showing mushroom shapes and human figures with mushroom heads are consistent with some level of reverence for mushrooms in this part of the world many thousands of years ago.[9] The mushroom consumed in Russia was the fly agaric, *Amanita muscaria*, whose psychoactive ingredient, muscimol, retains its potency after passing through the kidneys. Stories about the use of mushrooms by the Koryak were popularized in the nineteenth century by Mordecai Cubitt Cooke, whose book *The Seven Sisters of Sleep: Popular History of the Seven Prevailing Narcotics of the World* was published in 1860.[10] Cooke was a bizarre figure, even in the company of other celebrated mushroom experts. He authored hundreds of books and articles on fungi, was a founding member of the British Mycological Society, and pursued a tragic domestic life in which he made ruinous financial decisions and fathered seven (possibly eight) children with his adopted stepdaughter.[11]

Cooke's book was a possible source of inspiration for Alice's encounter with the caterpillar and his mushroom in *Alice's Adventures in Wonderland*. Her shrinkage after drinking from a bottle labelled 'DRINK ME' is reminiscent of the changes in size perception caused by muscimol and recalls the unappetizing custom of the Koryak. Charles Dodgson, whose pen-name was Lewis Carroll, must have read about the effects of the fly agaric in *The Seven Sisters of Sleep* or in an earlier account of mushroom intoxication. Hallucinatory worlds in which mushrooms tower over travellers are described in other Victorian novels, including *Voyage au centre de la terre* (1864), by Jules Verne, and *Etidorhpa* (Aphrodite spelled backwards, published in 1895) by John Uri Lloyd, brother of the Cincinnati mycologist Curtis Gates Lloyd.[12]

Muscimol has different effects on the central nervous system to psilocybin.[13] When it crosses the blood–brain barrier it binds to a receptor in the nervous system called GABA$_A$. The GABA$_A$ receptor is assembled as a unit of five protein sub-units in the cell membrane that create a pore that admits chloride ions. Influx of chloride ions through the pore is key to the flow of electrical impulses in the nervous system. When a neurotransmitter

Mordecai Cubitt Cooke sitting in the middle of the front row of the founding members of the British Mycological Society in 1895.

molecule called gamma-aminobutyric acid, abbreviated as GABA, binds to the receptor it stops the flow of chloride. This has the immediate effect of inhibiting nervous activity. Many drugs, including benzodiazepines used as sedatives, barbiturates and inhaled anaesthetics, enhance the effect of GABA by binding to various sites on the receptor. Alcohol is another psychoactive drug that works in this fashion, potentiating the natural effects of GABA. Muscimol has a more intimate relationship with the $GABA_A$ receptor than any of these compounds, placing itself in precisely the same site on the surface of the receptor as GABA. It is a perfect mimic.

GABA receptors are distributed throughout the brain and the effects of muscimol binding are apparent through alterations in information flow in the cerebral cortex (outer layers of brain), hippocampus (under the cortex) and cerebellum (back of the skull). Muscimol is classed as a sedative-hypnotic drug and affects emotions, memory retrieval and muscular coordination. It also produces dissociative effects in which users describe feelings of weightlessness, visual and auditory hallucinations and, like Alice, encounter size distortions in which small obstacles seem enormous.

It seems reasonable to assume that mushrooms produce psilocybin and muscimol because they perform useful functions that, ultimately, allow the fungus to keep producing spores. Two observations support this conclusion. First, they are fashioned from simple precursors called amino acids, whose structure is reorganized and augmented through a series of biochemical reactions that consume energy.[14] This 'anabolic' metabolic origin contrasts with the 'catabolic' formation of many metabolic wastes associated with the release of energy. The resulting levels of both psychotropic compounds vary from 0.2 to 2 per cent of the dry weight of the fruit body, which is similar to the concentration of the toxins in death cap mushrooms. A second line of evidence seems to clinch the case for the deliberate synthesis of psilocybin by fungi to meet a significant need. This comes from genetic studies showing that psilocybin synthesis has evolved repeatedly in different mushroom families. Muscimol synthesis is different. It was a one-off evolutionary innovation and is only found in *Amanita muscaria* and *Amanita pantherina*, the panther cap.

Figuring out what psilocybin and muscimol might do for a mushroom is an exercise in creative thinking because there have been no experiments that help us solve this question. Similarities between the nervous systems of all animals mean that both compounds will find the appropriate receptors in anything that eats fruit bodies containing psilocybin and muscimol. This zoological fact suggests that the likeliest function of these compounds is to upset nervous system function in insects and other invertebrates in ways that prevent them from destroying the mushroom. Things that make us hallucinate may also be effective at stunning insects and nematode worms. In the absence of further objective research, it seems likely that psilocybin and muscimol are pesticides. Their profound effect on human physiology is one of the more surprising illustrations of the noise of life. Rather than discouraging consumption by humans, these compounds have had the opposite effect of serving as a powerful attractant for disciples of 'shrooms'. On the other hand, the properties of *Psilocybe cubensis* have driven its geographical spread through cultivation.

These pharmacological facts have little bearing on the cultural significance of magic mushrooms. Worshipping psilocybes seems quite reasonable when compared with the human devotion to entirely invisible entities throughout history. At least mushrooms exist. The problems come when people convince themselves that distortions in perception caused by fungi help us to understand some greater truths about our place in the universe. People who have enjoyed the magic mushroom experience often use the language of religious rapture to describe their feelings. Feeling 'closer to God' is a common sentiment in controlled experiments with psilocybin. This is interesting because it demonstrates that the widespread experience of a phantom presence, or 'personal angel', can be provoked, or heightened, by a single molecule produced in the flesh of a mushroom.

To an atheist, this supports the conclusion that all religious experience has a rather straightforward pharmacological basis. To the believer, magic mushrooms may be seen as facilitators that enhance one's awareness of God. The second response is exemplified by the Aztecs' regard for psilocybes as the flesh of the gods. Deities come and go with the decline and fall of civilizations, but the essence of faith remains the same. The most significant message offered by psychotropic mushrooms is that our complicated nervous systems are constructed from the same components we find in flies.

# sixteen
# Mushroom Conservation

The future abundance of mushrooms is linked to human population growth and its impact on forest clearance, agriculture and the overarching phenomenon of climate change. It is difficult to evaluate the threat to individual mushroom species from this rapid transformation of the global environment. We can begin by looking at the science of animal conservation for guidance. Animals are ranked on a scale that runs from least concern (Canada goose) to gone for ever (passenger pigeon). With a global population of wild Bengal tigers of fewer than 2,500, *Panthera tigris tigris* is classified as threatened.[1] Estimates of the number of individual tigers vary a good deal, but remote cameras are helping zoologists get closer to an accurate count. It is harder to census aquatic mammals such as endangered river dolphins, but at least the nature of the individual is clear. The definition of the individual fungus is more a matter of language and philosophy than science.

A fruit body is a reproductive organ formed by a larger colony. A weekend count of a thousand fruit bodies with red caps and white spots in a few hectares of woodland says something about the vitality of fly agarics. But if all of these mushrooms come from ten mycelia it might be more sensible to say that there are ten fly agarics in the study area. A mushroom does not count as a separate organism. The mushroom life cycle complicates the issue further, because two colonies have to combine their resources before fruiting can take place. Some large colonies can even develop into genetic mosaics as multiple mating reactions occur at different points across their territories. Are we dealing with a population of networked individuals in a colony of this kind?

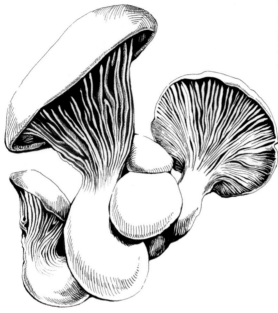

The critically endangered white ferula mushroom, *Pleurotus nebrodensis.*

Genetic diversity is another important consideration for the conservation of fungi. The obvious effect of mushroom picking on spore dispersal and its knock-on effect upon the genetic variation among mycelia is one of the reasons for being more cautious about the commercial harvesting of wild mushrooms. Genetic diversity is a big deal for animal conservation too. The limited genetic variation among tigers in parts of their range in Asia may be a greater long-term challenge for the species than the fact that there are so few animals.

With all of these considerations bubbling away in the minds of scientists, the International Union for the Conservation of Nature (IUCN) made a landmark decision in 2006 to list one mushroom species as critically endangered. The celebrity fungus is the white ferula mushroom, *Pleurotus nebrodensis*, which grows in an area of 100 square km in the northern part of Sicily and nowhere else.[2] This wild mushroom has been picked for centuries and today alarmingly few fruit bodies reach maturity before they are gathered. The white ferula mushroom is the black rhinoceros of mycology – both species are one notch up the scale (in the wrong direction) from the endangered Bengal tiger. Recognition of the precarious nature of the rhinoceros in the 1970s led to efforts to stabilize and rebuild populations by enforcing laws against poaching. The IUCN listing of *Pleurotus* has helped activists to introduce regulations against picking the mushroom in Sicily.

Because the fungus is not exported, there is no analogy to be drawn with international legislation to ban the trade in rhino horns, but the special biology of the mushroom has inspired another conservation approach.[3] The white ferula mushroom gets its name from its mycorrhizal association with a plant in the celery family whose Latin name is *Cachrys ferulacea*. This symbiotic relationship has led researchers to inoculate *Cachrys* roots with the mycelium in an effort to increase the number of fruiting colonies. *Pleurotus nebrodensis* is related to the edible king oyster mushroom, *Pleurotus eryngii*, whose cultivation on organic waste provides a model for keeping white ferula going

Ink cap mushrooms in dewy grass.

in captivity. Farming the endangered mushroom is comparable to breeding rhinos and tigers in zoos.

Listing one among the many thousands of mushrooms as critically endangered may encourage the idea that fungi are doing fine at a time of extraordinary threats to the survival of the more eye-catching animal species. This is a mistake. Like everything else in nature, mushrooms would be much better off today without us. The effect of human disturbance on biodiversity is so colossal in places where the most people live that it is not mentioned. Woodland around the nuclear power plant at Chernobyl is teeming with wildlife, albeit highly radioactive, for the simple reason that humans have stayed away since 1986. The mere presence of humans is, undeniably, much worse for the rest of life than the meltdown and explosion of a nuclear reactor.[4]

The impact of habitat preservation on mushrooms is quite obvious. Down House in Kent, where Charles Darwin lived for forty years, is part of Britain's National Heritage Collection. The lawns around the house are an example of old, unimproved grassland. More than two hundred species of mushroom have been recorded on Darwin's lawn.[5] Windsor Great Park is another, much larger, unimproved property that is celebrated for its variety of mushrooms. The contrast between these diversity hotspots and 'improved' grassland is stark. The same thing goes for the lawn surrounding my home in Ohio. Although the number of fungi that fruit on my property is not very impressive, it is an island of biodiversity compared with my neighbour's grass, which is subjected to regular dousing with chemical fertilizers. Soggy lawns decorated with mushrooms illustrate the habitat preservation part of the conservation strategy.

Controlled harvesting, the other arm of most conservation plans, is a more complicated issue for mycologists. Sustainable levels of mushroom picking have not been established and the effectiveness of licensing systems is untested. With some mushroom lovers arguing against any form of legal protection for fungi that transforms pickers into poachers, it is easy to see why the future of wild populations of the most valuable mushrooms is uncertain.

Climate change may prove an overwhelming challenge for conservation efforts, even in bioreserves that have been protected from any direct human influence. The effect of planetary warming on mushroom populations is difficult to forecast, particularly when associated changes in rainfall patterns will have a huge impact on fungi. More data would be helpful. The best records of fruiting patterns come from southwest England and show that the length of the autumn mushroom season has more than doubled since the 1950s.[6] This behaviour correlates with the upward trend in summer temperatures and increased rainfall in autumn. Some mushrooms that used to fruit once a year, particularly the wood-decomposing species, have begun emerging in the autumn *and* in the spring. The opposite effect has been seen in Norway, where warming is associated with a delay in the appearance of mushrooms and shortening of the fruiting season.[7] It is impossible to know whether or not these observations reflect long-term shifts in reproductive behaviour, but it is troubling that these changes have occurred so quickly. If future temperature and rainfall patterns prolong the annual period of mycelial growth, rates of wood decomposition are going to accelerate. Conversely, reduced rates of decay might be expected from the results of the Norwegian study. Either way, these deviations from the 'normal' schedule of fungal growth are likely to affect soil fertility in woodlands, plant development and the availability of food for wild animals.

Another feature of mushroom biology helps to illustrate the surprising intimacy between the lives of these fungi and our planet's habitability. The mechanism that launches mushroom spores from gills was described in Chapter Two. It involves the lightning-fast movement of a tiny drop of fluid over the surface of the spore. The drop is called Buller's drop in memory of A.H.R. Buller, the brilliant pioneer of fungi research. After the spores are released and are blown around in the air, Buller's drop evaporates. It was discovered recently that water will condense on the dry particle again if it is exposed to humid air: Buller's drop reappears, as if by magic.[8] This facility to attract and lose water could be critical in allowing spores to participate in the genesis of raindrops. Astonishing numbers of spores accumulate in the atmosphere above wet habitats like rainforests where the ground is festooned with mushrooms of every shape, size and colour. In this mycological paradise, mushroom spores may stimulate rainfall when they disperse above the trees.

This coupling between mycology and rainfall is not proven, but the physics work perfectly when the spores are exposed to the appropriate environmental conditions in the laboratory. It is supported by research on atmospheric chemistry, which allows us to estimate the gargantuan number of spores dispersed in the atmosphere every year. If these particles were spread evenly over the surface of the earth, every square millimetre would be populated with one thousand spores. The scarcity of spores over oceans and their concentration above the most productive ecosystems on land makes it most likely that mushrooms could affect the dynamics of cloud formation and rainfall over forests. This encourages the idea that a positive feedback mechanism may operate in which mushroom growth is supported by rainfall, and spores released from these mushrooms stimulate more precipitation. The operation of this cycle would be vulnerable to the sort of climate-related changes in fruiting behaviour reported in Europe. Disturbance to fungi may affect the rainfall patterns that sustained them in the first place, and the resulting slump in mycelial growth will depress the next round of fruiting, until the mushrooms are no more.

Because civilization continues to depend on the viability of forests and grasslands, the fate of humanity is bound up with the roles of mushrooms in mycorrhizal associations with plants and as the prime agents of wood decay. If we fail to protect the ecosystems in which mushrooms flourish, and that these fungi help to sustain, wild fruitings will become less common. The immediate significance of this will be lost on people who have little appreciation of the organisms described in this book. This is an error of their judgement, because the disappearance of fungi would forecast unprecedented trouble for our species.

Our ancestors evolved in forest ecosystems sustained by mycorrhizal mushrooms that partnered with plants, and saprotrophic mushrooms that kept the soils fertile by recycling biological waste. During the tens of thousands of years of human evolution, the mycelia of these fungi energized food webs in the leaf litter and purified the water that percolated through the woodlands. We need mushrooms to keep doing these things. If things get too hot, our numbers will drop from billions to millions. This human catastrophe will allow the rest of nature to reboot as she has always done after a big shakeup. Plants will create new cover and biological diversity will rebound. And whether we are here or have extinguished ourselves, gilled mushrooms will cast their spores into the breeze and mist the blue skies of Earth so pregnant with clouds.

# Timeline

| | |
|---|---|
| 1 billion years ago | Fungi and animals evolve as separate groups from a common aquatic ancestor with single cells |
| 500 million years ago | Basidiomycete fungi, which include mushrooms, follow separate evolutionary path from the ascomycetes |
| 400 million years ago | Date of oldest-known fossils of fungi |
| 330 million years ago | Fossilization of filamentous cells whose structure resembles the filamentous hyphae of mushroom colonies |
| 290 million years ago | Origin of major groups of mushroom-forming fungi and development of mechanisms for decomposing wood containing lignin |
| 100 million years ago | Oldest gilled mushrooms fossilized in amber |
| 15–50 million years ago | Age range of bird's nest fungi found fossilized in amber |
| 3–5 million years ago | Age of fossil earth-stars |
| 8,000 years ago | Putative symbols of mushroom worship painted in the Algerian Sahara |

| | |
|---|---|
| 7,000 years ago | Earliest written records of mushroom consumption and poisoning in Greece |
| 5,000–4,000 years ago | Neolithic stone circles erected in Europe that may have been inspired by fairy rings |
| 2,000 years ago | Mushrooms vilified by classical writers, but become a treasured part of Roman cuisine |
| 1200s | Earliest description of shiitake mushroom cultivation in China |
| 1500s | Conquistadors discover ritual use of hallucinogenic mushrooms by Aztecs |
| 1558 | Pietro Andrea Mattioli publishes earliest illustrations of identifiable mushroom species |
| 1588 | First observation of mushroom spores by Giambattista della Porta, who described 'seeds [spores], very small and black' |
| 1601 | Groundbreaking monograph describing more than a hundred mushroom species published by Carolus Clusius |
| 1665 | Publication of Robert Hooke's *Micrographia* showing first images of microscopic fungi and describing the anatomy of mushrooms |

| | |
|---|---|
| 1675 | Publication of Franciscus van Sterbeeck's *Theatrum fungorum*, the first book devoted wholly to mushrooms |
| 1729 | Publication of Pier Antonio Micheli's *Nova plantarum genera*, which reported experiments on mushroom spores that refuted spontaneous generation |
| 1700s | Cultivation of meadow mushrooms on animal manure becomes widespread in Europe |
| 1820s | Christiaan Hendrik Persoon and Elias Magnus Fries develop competing systems for classifying fungi |
| 1853 | Anton de Bary publishes first textbook on mycology |
| 1872 | Oscar Brefeld develops method for growing pure cultures of fungi on gelatin (based on work by earlier investigators) |
| 1909–34 | Publication of six volumes of A.H.R. Buller's *Researches on Fungi*, the great treatise on experimental mycology |
| 1969 | Fungi classified in their own kingdom by Robert Whittaker |
| 1970s | Studies on the structure of fungi using electron microscopy |

| | |
|---|---|
| 1980s | Molecular genetic techniques used to study the evolutionary relationships between different groups of fungi and the introduction of molecular biological research on fungal development |
| 2008 | Entire genome of *Laccaria bicolor* sequenced, marking the completion of the first genome project for a mushroom |

# References

## Introduction

1 R. Roeh and K. Chadwick, eds, *Decomposition: An Anthology of Fungi-inspired Poems* (Sandpoint, ID, 2010), p. 78.

## 1 Mushroom Superstition

1 A.H.R. Buller, 'The Fungus Lore of the Greeks and Romans', *Transactions of the British Mycological Society*, V (1914–16), pp. 21–66; F. M. Dugan, *Fungi in the Ancient World* (St Paul, MN, 2008).

2 Pliny the Elder, *Natural History*, Book 22, XLVII, 96–7, *Loeb Classical Library*, 392 (Cambridge, MA, 1951), pp. 360–61.

3 The phrase is attributed to Basil Willey (1897–1978), professor of English literature at Cambridge.

4 B. Spooner and T. Læssø, 'The Folklore of "Gasteromycetes"', *Mycologist*, VIII (1994), pp. 119–23.

5 B. A. Oso, 'Mushrooms in Yoruba Mythology and Medical Practices', *Economic Botany*, XXXI (1977), pp. 367–71.

6 Anonymous ('A lady'), 'The Fairy Ring', in *The Harebell: A Book of Poems* (Liverpool, 1863).

7 E. Spenser, *The Shepheardes Calender* (London, 1579); for an excellent modern edition, see E. Spenser, *The Shorter Poems*, ed. R. A. McCabe (London, 1999).

8 T. Baker, 'The Origin of the Word "Mushroom"', *Mycologist*, III (1989), pp. 88–90.

9 Pliny, *Natural History*, Book 22, XLVI, 94, pp. 358–9.

10 T. Baker, 'The Word "Toadstool" in Britain', *Mycologist*, IV (1990), pp. 25–9.

11 A. Letcher, *Shroom: A Cultural History of the Magic Mushroom* (London, 2006).

12 J. Ramsbottom, *Mushrooms and Toadstools: A Study of the Activities of Fungi* (London, 1953).

13  G. E. Rumphius, *The Ambonese Herbal*, trans. E. M. Beekman, vol. V (New Haven, CT, 2010), p. 249.

## 2 Mushroom Science

1  G. C. Ainsworth, *An Introduction to the History of Mycology* (Cambridge, 1976).
2  N. P. Money, *Mushroom* (New York and Oxford, 2011), pp. 5–6.
3  A. Pringle et al., 'The Captured Launch of a Ballistospore', *Mycologia*, XCVII (2005), pp. 866–71.
4  A.H.R. Buller, *Researches on Fungi*, vols I–VI (London, 1909–34), vol. VII (Toronto, 1950).
5  U. Kües and M. Navarro-González, 'How Do Agaricomycetes Shape their Fruiting Bodies? 1. Morphological Aspects of Development', *Fungal Biology Reviews*, XXIX (2015), pp. 63–97.

## 3 Mushroom Diversity

1  G. E. Hutchinson, 'Homage to Santa Rosalia, or Why are there So Many Kinds of Animals?', *American Naturalist*, XCIII (1959), pp. 145–59.
2  M.W.F. Fischer and N. P. Money, 'Why Mushrooms Form Gills: Efficiency of the Lamellate Morphology', *Fungal Biology*, CXIV (2010), pp. 57–63.

## 4 Mushroom Evolution

1  T. N. Taylor, M. Krings and E. L. Taylor, *Fossil Fungi* (Amsterdam, 2015).
2  D. S. Hibbett, 'A Phylogenetic Overview of the Agaricomycotina', *Mycologia*, XCVIII (2006), pp. 917–25.
3  D. S. Hibbett et al., 'A Higher-level Phylogenetic Classification of the Fungi', *Mycological Research*, CXI (2007), pp. 509–47.
4  R. Deering, F. Dong, D. Rambo and N. P. Money, 'Airflow Patterns Around Mushrooms and their Relationship to Spore Dispersal', *Mycologia*, XCIII (2001), pp. 732–6.

## 5 Mushroom Sexuality

1  The first report of an enormous mycelium described an *Armillaria* mycelium in Michigan: M. L. Smith, J. N. Bruhn and J. B. Anderson,

'The Fungus *Armillaria bulbosa* is Among the Largest and Oldest Living Organisms', *Nature*, CCCLVI (1992), pp. 428–31. This mycelium was eclipsed by the monster in Oregon, described by C. L. Schmitt and M. L. Tatum, 'The Malheur National Forest: Location of the World's Largest Living Organism [The Humongous Fungus]', United States Department of Agriculture Forest Service, Pacific Northwest Region (2008).

2   More information on the mating systems of mushrooms is provided by S. C. Watkinson, L. Boddy and N. P. Money, *The Fungi*, 3rd edn (Amsterdam, 2016).

3   A.H.R. Buller, *Researches on Fungi*, vol. IV (London, 1931), pp. 117–20; N. P. Money and J. P. Ravishankar, 'Biomechanics of Stipe Elongation in the Basidiomycete *Coprinopsis cinerea*', *Mycological Research*, CIX (2005), pp. 628–35.

4   The story of the contributions to our understanding of the mushroom life cycle by W. G. Smith and E. M. Wakefield is told in N. P. Money, *Mushroom* (New York and Oxford, 2011), pp. 13–15.

## 6 Mushroom Function

1   If we assume that the formation of gills increases the surface area by the same factor for both species, we can compare the area of the circle underneath the caps ($\pi r^2$) to estimate the number of smaller mushrooms with an equivalent surface area to the larger species. In the case described in Chapter Six, the underside of the 9 cm cap has an area of 64 cm$^2$ and the bottom of the smaller mushroom has an area of 0.2 cm$^2$. This means that 320 smaller mushrooms support the same area as a single larger fruit body. The precise surface area for spore production in these species is affected by differences in gill arrangements and the relative size of the connection between the stem and cap. For this reason, I rounded the estimate of the number of small fruit bodies to a single significant figure in the text.

2   X. Noblin, S. Yang and J. Dumais, 'Surface Tension Propulsion of Fungal Spores', *Journal of Experimental Biology*, CCXII (2009), pp. 2835–43.

3   A. Pringle et al., 'The Captured Launch of a Ballistospore', *Mycologia*, XCVII (2005), pp. 866–71.

4   J. L. Stolze-Rybczynski et al., 'Adaptation of the Spore Discharge Mechanism in the Basidiomycota', *PLOS ONE*, IV/1: e4163 doi:10.1371/journal.pone.0004163 (2009).

5   J. Husher et al., 'Evaporative Cooling of Mushrooms', *Mycologia*, XCI (1999), pp. 351–2.

6   E. Dressaire, L. Yamada and M. Roper, 'Mushroom Spore Dispersal by Convectively-driven Winds', *Proceedings of the National Academy of Sciences*, CXIII (2016), pp. 2833–8.

7   A. G. Oliveira et al., 'Circadian Control Sheds Light on Fungal Bioluminescence', *Current Biology*, XXV (2015), pp. 964–8.

8   M. O. Hassett et al., 'Splash and Grab: Biomechanics of Peridiole Ejection and Function of the Funicular Cord in Bird's Nest Fungi', *Fungal Biology*, CXVII (2013), pp. 708–14.

## 7 Mushroom Experts

1   L. G. Goldsborough, 'Reginald Buller: The Poet-scientist of the Mushroom City', *Manitoba History*, XLVII (2004), pp. 17–41.

2   C. McIlvaine, *One Thousand American Fungi: How to Select and Cook the Edible; How to Distinguish and Avoid the Poisonous* (Indianapolis, IN, 1900).

3   N. P. Money, *Mr Bloomfield's Orchard: The Mysterious World of Mushrooms, Molds, and Mycologists* (New York and Oxford, 2002), pp. 95–103.

4   See www.lloydlibrary.org.

5   N. P. Money, 'Cecil Terence Ingold (1905–2010)', *Nature*, CDLXV (2010), p. 1025.

6   S. Branco and E. Vellinga, 'Gender Balance in Mycology', *Inoculum*, LXVI (2015), pp. 1–4.

7   N. P. Money, 'Beatrix Potter: Victorian Mycologist', *Fungi*, II/4 (2009), pp. 63–4.

## 8 Mushroom Ecology

1   There is no accessible comprehensive book on mycorrhizas, but these relationships receive detailed coverage in S. C. Watkinson, L. Boddy and N. P. Money, *The Fungi*, 3rd edn (Amsterdam, 2016), pp. 205–28.

2   J. N. Klironomos and M. M. Hart, 'Food-web Dynamics: Animal Nitrogen Swap for Plant Carbon', *Nature*, CDX (2001), pp. 651–2.

3   F. Martin et al., 'The Genome of *Laccaria bicolor* Provides Insights into Mycorrhizal Symbiosis', *Nature*, CDLII (2008), pp. 88–92.

4   Y.-C. Dai and B.-K. Cui, 'Fomitiporia ellipsoidea has the Largest Fruit Body Among the Fungi', *Fungal Biology*, cvx (2011), pp. 813–14.

## 9  Mushroom Parasites

1   H. C. Evans, 'Cacao Diseases in the Americas: Myths and Misnomers', *Fungi*, v/4 (2012), pp. 29–35.
2   N. Mondiet, M.-P. Dubois and M.-A. Selosse, 'The Enigmatic *Squamanita odorata* (Agaricales, Basidiomycota) is Parasitic on *Hebeloma mesophaeum*', *Mycological Research*, clxvii (2007), pp. 59–602.
3   H. Luo et al., '*Coprinus comatus* Damages Nematode Cuticles Mechanically with Spiny Balls and Produces Potent Toxins to Immobilize Nematodes', *Applied and Environmental Microbiology*, lxiii (2007), pp. 3916–23.
4   D. Williamson et al., 'A Case of Infection Caused by the Basidiomycete *Phellinus undulatus*', *Journal of Medical Microbiology*, lx (2011), pp. 256–8. Other case reports of human infections by basidiomycetes are cited in this paper.
5   R. Barnes and R. Richardson, 'Fungi – Forgotten Foes', *Bulletin of the Royal College of Physicians*, 167 (2014), pp. 161–2. The estimate is based on the published figure of 1.5 million deaths per year caused by invasive fungal diseases, which equates to 4,100 deaths every day, or 170 per hour.

## 10  Mushroom Picking

1   A selection of mushroom guidebooks and websites is provided in the Further Reading and Associations and Websites sections.
2   N. P. Money, *The Amoeba in the Room: Lives of the Microbes* (Oxford and New York, 2014).
3   W. E. Schlosser and K. A. Blatner, 'The Wild Edible Mushroom Industry of Washington, Oregon and Idaho: A 1992 Survey', *Journal of Forestry*, xciii (1995), pp. 31–6.
4   W. S. Sun and J. Y. Xu, 'Cultivation of Edible Fungi has Become One of the Backbone Industries in Rural Economy of China', *Edible Fungi of China*, xviii (1999), pp. 5–6; E. R. Boa, 'Wild Edible Fungi: A Global Overview of their Use and Importance to People', *Non-Wood Forest Products*, xvii (Rome, 2004).
5   N. P. Money, 'Why Picking Wild Mushrooms May be Bad Behavior', *Mycological Research*, cix (2005), pp. 131–5.

6   S. Egli et al., 'Mushroom Picking Does Not Impair Future Harvests: Results of a Long-term Study in Switzerland', *Biological Conservation*, CXXIX (2006), pp. 271–6.

## 11  Mushroom Growing

1   S.-T. Chang and P. G. Miles, *Mushrooms: Cultivation, Nutritional Value, Medicinal Effect, and Environmental Impact* (Boca Raton, FL, 2004); P. Stamets, *Growing Gourmet and Medicinal Mushrooms* (Berkeley, CA, 2000).
2   Y. Zhang et al., 'Edible Mushroom Cultivation for Food Security and Rural Development in China: Bio-innovation, Technological Dissemination and Marketing', *Sustainability*, VI (2014), pp. 2961–73.
3   N. P. Money, *Mushroom* (New York and Oxford, 2011), pp. 97–106.

## 12  Mushroom Cooking

1   Hank Shaw, 'Chanterelles in All Their Forms', http://honest-food.net, 5 November 2010.
2   D. Badham, *A Treatise on the Esculent Funguses of England: Containing an Account of Their Classical History, Uses, Characters, Development, Structure, Nutritious Properties, Modes of Cooking and Preserving, &c.* (London, 1847), p. viii.
3   Ovid, *Fasti*, Loeb Classical Library, 253, trans. J. G. Frazer, revd G. P. Goold, Book IV, line 697 (Cambridge, MA, 1989), pp. 240–41.
4   G. Brown, I. R. Hall and A. Zambonelli, *Taming the Truffle: The History, Lore, and Science of the Ultimate Mushroom* (Portland, OR, 2008).

## 13  Mushroom Poisons

1   Juvenal, *The Sixteen Satires*, trans. P. Green, Satire V, lines 147–8 (London, 2014), p. 37.
2   Seneca, *The Apolocyntosis of the Divine Claudius*, trans. J. P. Sullivan (London, 1986), pp. 223–4, included in this Penguin edition with Petronius, *The Satyricon*; V. J. Marmion and T.E.J. Wiedmann, 'The Death of Claudius', *Journal of the Royal Society of Medicine*, XCV (2002), pp. 260–61.
3   D. R. Benjamin, *Mushrooms: Poisons and Panaceas – A Handbook for Naturalists, Mycologists, and Physicians* (New York, 1995).
4   B. A. Bunyard, 'The Real Story Behind Increased *Amanita* Poisonings in North America', *Fungi*, VIII/3 (2015), pp. 6–9.

5  N. P. Money, *Mushroom* (New York and Oxford, 2011), pp. 117–19.

6  D. H. Lawrence, 'How Beastly the Bourgeois Is', in *The Complete Poems of D. H. Lawrence*, collected and ed. V. de S. Pinto and W. Roberts (New York, 1971).

7  E. Heimer, *Der Giftpilz* (Nuremburg, 1938). The book's publisher, Julius Streicher, was executed for his crimes against humanity in 1946.

## 14  Mushroom Medicines

1  This chapter is adapted from a review article published by the author: N. P. Money, 'Are Mushrooms Medicinal?', *Fungal Biology*, cxx (2016), pp. 449–53.

2  K. Jones, *Shiitake: The Healing Mushroom* (Rochester, vt, 1995).

3  'Lentinan', www.mskcc.org, 24 August 2015; the Memorial Sloan Kettering Cancer Center in New York provides an excellent objective analysis of hundreds of 'herbs, botanicals, and other products' that have purported uses in the treatment of cancer. Each webpage dedicated to a medicinal mushroom species has an up-to-date list of references to clinical studies.

4  M. Zhou et al., 'Cause-specific Mortality for 240 Causes in China during 1990–2013: A Systematic Subnational Analysis for the Global Burden of Disease Study 2013', *The Lancet* (October 2015), DOI: 10.1016/s0140-6736(15)00551-6.

5  A.-R. Harrison-Dunn, 'A Global Look at Supplements on the Rise', www.nutraingredients.com, 10 March 2014.

6  'Reishi Mushroom', www.mskcc.org, 30 December 2015.

7  'Coriolus Versicolor', www.mskcc.org, 12 December 2014.

8  A. Solzhenitsyn, *Cancer Ward*, trans. N. Bethell and D. Burg (New York, 1969), pp. 135–54.

9  'Chaga Mushroom', www.mskcc.org, 22 December 2015.

10  'Maitake', www.mskcc.org, 2 April 2015.

11  References in Money, 'Are Mushrooms Medicinal?'

12  See www.fungi.com; the quotes were obtained from the website in December 2015.

13  B.-J. Ma et al., 'Hericenones and Erinacines: Stimulators of Nerve Growth Factor (NGF) Biosynthesis in *Hericium erinaceus*', *Mycology*, 1 (2010), pp. 92–8.

14  Dr Bonker Medicine Co., Chicago, 'Dr Bonker's Celebrated Egyptian Oil', www.bonkersinstitute.org/medshow/bonkermed.html, accessed

7 June 2015; W. H. Helfand, 'President's Address: Samuel Solomon and The Cordial Balm of Gilead', *Pharmacy in History*, xxxi (1989), pp. 151–9.

15  S. C. Watkinson, L. Boddy and N. P. Money, *The Fungi*, 3rd edn (Amsterdam, 2016), pp. 418–20.

## 15  Mushroom Hallucinogens

1  P. Stamets, *Psilocybin Mushrooms of the World: An Identification Guide* (Berkeley, CA, 1996).

2  F. Tylš, T. Páleníček and J. Horáček, 'Psilocybin – Summary of Knowledge and New Perspectives', *European Neuropsychopharmacology*, xxiv (2014), pp. 342–56.

3  R. L. Carhart-Harris et al., 'Neural Correlates of the Psychedelic State as Determined by fMRI Studies with Psilocybin', *Proceedings of the National Academy of Sciences*, cix (2012), pp. 2138–43.

4  J.-D. Lajoux, *The Rock Paintings of Tassili* (Cleveland, OH, 1963).

5  B. P. Akers et al., 'A Prehistoric Mural in Spain Depicting Neurotropic *Psilocybe* Mushrooms?', *Economic Botany*, lxv (2011), pp. 121–8.

6  J. Ramsbottom, *Mushrooms and Toadstools: A Study of the Activities of Fungi* (London, 1953), pp. 46–7.

7  A. Letcher, *Shroom: A Cultural History of the Magic Mushroom* (London, 2006), pp. 72–7.

8  P. J. von Strahlenberg, *An Histori-geographical Description of the North and Eastern Parts of Europe and Asia* (London, 1736), p. 397.

9  N. N. Dikov, *Mysteries in the Rocks of Ancient Chukotka (Petroglyphs of Pegtymel)*, trans. Richard L. Bland (Anchorage, AK, 1999); available at www.nps.gov/parkhistory/online_books/bela/chukotka.pdf.

10  M. C. Cooke, *The Seven Sisters of Sleep: Popular History of the Seven Prevailing Narcotics of the World* (London, 1860).

11  M. P. English, *Mordecai Cubitt Cooke: Victorian Naturalist, Mycologist, Teacher and Eccentric* (Bristol, 1987).

12  J. Verne, *Voyage au centre de la terre* (Paris, 1864), trans. F. A. Malleson as *Journey to the Centre of the Earth* (London, 1871); J. U. Lloyd, *Etidorpha* (Cincinnati, OH, 1895).

13  D. Michelot and L. M. Melendez-Howell, '*Amanita muscaria*: Chemistry, Biology, Toxicology, and Ethnomycology', *Mycological Research*, cvii (2003), pp. 131–46.

14 P. P. Wieczorek et al., 'Bioactive Alkaloids of Hallucinogenic Mushrooms', in A.-u-Rahman, ed., *Studies in Natural Products Chemistry*, XLVI (Amsterdam, 2015), pp. 133–68; J. Velíšek, J. Davídek and K. Cejpek, 'Biosynthesis of Food Constituents: Natural Pigments, Part I – A Review', *Czech Journal of Food Science*, XXV (2007), pp. 291–315.

## 16 Mushroom Conservation

1 IUCN Red List of Threatened Species, 'Panthera tigris ssp. tigris (Bengal Tiger)', www.iucnredlist.org, accessed 7 June 2016.

2 See IUCN Red List of Threatened Species, 'Pleurotus nebrodensis (White Ferula Mushroom)', www.iucnredlist.org, accessed 7 June 2016.

3 M. L. Gargano, G. I. Zervakis and G. Venturella, eds, *Pleurotus nebrodensis: A Very Special Mushroom* (Sharjah, UAE, 2013).

4 T. G. Deryabina et al., 'Long-term Census Data Reveal Abundant Wildlife Populations at Chernobyl', *Current Biology*, XXV (2015), pp. R824–R826.

5 The house, garden and grounds of Down House in the London Borough of Bromley are under the guardianship of English Heritage: see www.english-heritage.org.uk.

6 A. C. Gange et al., 'Rapid and Recent Changes in Fungal Fruiting Patterns', *Science*, CCCXVI (2007), p. 71.

7 H. Kauserud et al., 'Mushroom Fruiting and Climate Change', *Proceedings of the National Academy of Sciences*, CV (2008), pp. 3811–14.

8 M. O. Hassett, M.W.F. Fischer and N. P. Money, 'Mushrooms as Rainmakers: How Spores Act as Nuclei for Raindrops', PLOS ONE, X/10 (2015), e0140407. doi: 10.1371/journal.pone.0140407.

# Further Reading

## Mushroom Books Written for Non-specialists

Bone, E., *Mycophilia: Revelations from the Weird World of Mushrooms* (Emmaus, PA, 2013)

Money, N. P., *Mr Bloomfield's Orchard: The Mysterious World of Mushrooms, Molds, and Mycologists* (New York and Oxford, 2002)

—, *Mushroom* (New York and Oxford, 2011)

## Mushroom Biology

Alexopoulos, C. J., C. W. Mims and M. M. Blackwell, *Introductory Mycology*, 4th edn (New York, 1996)

Money, N. P., *Fungi: A Very Short Introduction* (Oxford, 2016)

Watkinson, S. C., L. Boddy and N. P. Money, *The Fungi*, 3rd edn (Amsterdam, 2016)

Webster J., and R.W.S. Weber, *Introduction to Fungi*, 3rd edn (Cambridge, 2007)

## Illustrated Guidebooks

Lincoff, G. A., G. H. Lincoff and C. Nehring, *National Audubon Field Guide to North American Mushrooms* (New York, 1981)

McKnight, K., and V. McKnight, *Peterson Field Guide Series: A Field Guide to Mushrooms of North America* (Boston, MA, 1998)

Petersen, J. H., *The Kingdom of Fungi* (Princeton, NJ, 2012)

Phillips, R., *Mushrooms and Other Fungi of North America* (Buffalo, NY, 2010)

Sterry, P., and B. Hughes, *Collins Complete British Mushrooms and Toadstools: The Essential Photograph Guide to Britain's Fungi* (London, 2009)

# Associations and Websites

THE AUSTRALASIAN MYCOLOGICAL SOCIETY
www.australasianmycologicalsociety.com

THE BRITISH MYCOLOGICAL SOCIETY
www.britmycolsoc.org.uk

THE MYCOLOGICAL SOCIETY OF AMERICA
www.msafungi.org

MYCOLOGICAL SOCIETY OF CHINA
www.mscfungi.org

THE MYCOLOGICAL SOCIETY OF JAPAN
www.mycology-jp.org/~msj7/index.html

THE NORTH AMERICAN MYCOLOGICAL ASSOCIATION
www.namyco.org

THE EUROPEAN MYCOLOGICAL ASOCIATION
and THE NORTHERN IRELAND FUNGUS GROUP
provide global listings of national and regional mycological societies:
www.euromould.org/links/socs.htm
www.nifg.org.uk/other_websites.htm

An independent magazine, *Fungi*, is a highly informative quarterly journal
on all things mycological:
www.fungimag.com

The Internet offers the richest source of mushroom images to help in identification. Here are a few of the best websites:

www.kingdomoffungi.com
www.mushroomexpert.com
www.mushroomobserver.org
www.rogersmushrooms.com

# Acknowledgements

The author wishes to thank Anna Heran, Curator at the Lloyd Library and Museum, for her expertise in scanning original sources from the outstanding collection of mycological books and periodicals in Cincinnati.

## Permissions

The author thanks Christine Boyka Kluge and Lost Horse Press in Sandpoint, Idaho, for permission to reprint her poem 'Toadstools'.

# Photo Acknowledgements

The author and publishers wish to express their thanks to the below sources of illustrative material and/or permission to reproduce it:

Photo AfriPics.com/Alamy: p. 45; photo Alamy Stock Photo: p. 160; photos by or courtesy of author: pp. 20, 68, 83, 114; from Giovanni A. Battarra, *Fungorum Agri Ariminenesis Historia a J. Antonio Battarra Compilata Aeneisque Tabulis Ornata* . . . (Faenza, 1755): pp. 112, 143; photo Beentree: p. 98 (this file is licensed under the Creative Commons Attribution-Share Alike 3.0 Unported license: any reader is free to share – to copy, distribute and transmit the work, or to remix – to adapt the work, under the following conditions: you must attribute the work in the manner specified by the author or licensor, but not in any way that suggests that they endorse you or your use of the work); photo Denis Benjamin: p. 118; from Émile Boudier, *Icones Mycologicæ, ou, Iconographie des Champignons de France* . . . vol. i (Paris, 1905): p. 33; from Oscar Brefeld, *Botanische Untersuchungen über Schimmelpilze* . . ., vol. vi (Leipzig, 1872): p. 106; from Pierre Bulliard, *Histoire de Champignons de la France* . . ., vol. iii (Paris, 1791): p. 113; from A. H. Reginald Buller, *Researches on Fungi*, vol. iv: *Further Observations on the Coprini, together with some Observations on Social Organisation and Sex in the Hymenomycetes* (London, 1931): p. 64; photo Ceekchean Tan © 123RF.COM: p. 149; photo Christinesgates/www.dreamstime.com: p. 128 (top); from M. C. Cooke, *Illustrations of British Fungi (Hymenomycetes) to serve as an atlas to the Handbook of British Fungi*, vol. iv (London, 1884–6): p. 61; from E.J.H. Corner, *A Monograph of Cantharelloid Fungi* (London, 1966), by permission of Oxford University Press: p. 29; photo © Jolanta Dabrowska/www.dreamstime.com: p. 108; photo © Ddkg/www.dreamstime.com: p. 151; from R. Dujarric de la Rivière, *Le Poison des Amanites Mortelles* (Paris, 1933): p. 138; photo Ananya Dechakhamphu © 123RF.COM: p. 48 (foot); © Dennis Kunkel Microscopy, Inc.: p. 60; photo Joshua C. Doty: p. 131; photo © Empire33/www.dreamstime.com: p. 140; photo Stephen Farhall © 123RF.

remix – to adapt the work, under the following conditions: you must attribute the work in the manner specified by the author or licensor, but not in any way that suggests that they endorse you or your use of the work); from Jean-Dominique Lajoux, *The Rock Paintings of Tassili . . .* (Cleveland, Ohio: The World Publishing Company, 1963): p. 158; photo Ellen Larsson, Göteborg University, Sweden: p. 92; from from C. G. Lloyd, *Mycological Notes*, LXXII [vol. VII, no. 6] (June, 1924): p. 89 (left); courtesy the Lloyd Library and Museum, Cincinnati: pp. 57, 87, 89 (left); photo Taylor Lockwood ('The Monarch of Mycological Photography'): p. 31; from Burton Orange Longyear, *Some Colorado Mushrooms* (Fort Collins, CO, 1915): p. 42; adapted from *McIlvainea: Journal of American Amateur Mycology*, vol. V (1982): p. 84; from David J. McLaughlin, Alan Beckett, and Kwon S. Yoon, 'Ultrastructure and Evolution of Ballistosporic Basidiospores', *Botanical Journal of the Linnean Society*, XCI/1–2 (1985): p. 74; from David MacRitchie, *Fians, Fairies and Picts* (London, 1893): p. 21; from Pietro A. Mattioli, *Petri Andreæ Matthioli [. . .] Commentarii secundo aucti, in libros sex Pedacii Dioscoridis Anazarbei, De medica materia . . .* (Venice, 1558): pp. 9, 27; from Pietro Antonio Micheli, *Nova Plantarum Genera juxta Tournefortii Methodum Disposita* (Florence, 1729): p. 30; photo Ivan Mikhaylov/ © 123RF. COM: p. 157; photo Dan Molter: p. 48 top (this file is licensed under the Creative Commons Attribution-Share Alike 3.0 Unported license: any reader is free to share – to copy, distribute and transmit the work, or to remix – to adapt the work, under the following conditions: you must attribute the work in the manner specified by the author or licensor, but not in any way that suggests that they endorse you or your use of the work); from Nicholas P. Money, *Carpet Monsters and Killer Spores: A Natural History of Toxic Mold* (New York, 2004): p. 99; photo Hajime Muraguchi, Akita Prefectural University, Japan: p. 66; photo © Nutthawit Wiangya © 123RF.COM: p. 154; photo Pasqueflower © 123RF.COM: p. 51; photo George Poinar: p. 54; photo David Pressland/MINDEN PICTURES: p. 44; © Trisha Previte 2016: p. 166; photo © Radub85, www.dreamstime.com: p. 75; photo Alan Rockefeller: p. 146 (this file is licensed under the Creative Commons Attribution-Share Alike 3.0 Unported license: any reader is free to share – to copy, distribute and transmit the work, or to remix – to adapt the work, under the following conditions: you must attribute the work in the manner specified by the author or licensor, but not in any way that suggests that they endorse you or your use of the work); from B. H. Shadduck, *The Toadstool*

# Index